CHRIST-CENTERED

Exposition

NT / COMMENTARY

AUTHORS **David Platt and Tony Merida**
SERIES EDITORS **David Platt, Daniel L. Akin, and Tony Merida**

CHRIST-CENTERED
Exposition

EXALTING JESUS IN

GALATIANS

HOLMAN
REFERENCE

NASHVILLE, TENNESSEE

SERIES DEDICATION

Dedicated to Adrian Rogers and John Piper. They have taught us to love the gospel of Jesus Christ, to preach the Bible as the inerrant Word of God, to pastor the church for which our Savior died, and to have a passion to see all nations gladly worship the Lamb.

—David Platt, Tony Merida, and Danny Akin
March 2013

TABLE OF CONTENTS

Galatians

DP = David Platt
TM = Tony Merida

ACKNOWLEDGMENTS

This commentary is evidence of God's grace in the lives of many brothers and sisters. I'm grateful for Imago Dei Church, who first heard these sermons. What an amazing privilege it was to expound Galatians each Sunday in our very young church plant. I am honored to pastor such an eager and encouraging fellowship. I'm also grateful to God for the elders that I get to serve with at IDC. I praise God for your friendship, wisdom, and leadership. I must also thank our Aspire guys, a group of interns that the elders meet with weekly. In addition to their other work, some of them have helped me edit this manuscript. Finally, to my bride Kimberly: What a joy it is to journey through this life with you, my dear companion. May God continue to sustain us, as we continue to boast in the cross of our Lord Jesus Christ. To Him be the glory forever.

Tony Merida

This commentary is the fruit of God's grace in the lives of many brothers and sisters. I am especially grateful to God for Cory Varden, who consistently and graciously serves alongside me, and David Burnette, who has taken my sermon manuscripts and edited them for my chapters of this commentary. I am ever grateful to God for Heather as well as Caleb, Joshua, Mara Ruth, and Isaiah; I am blessed beyond measure with the family He has entrusted to me. And I am deeply grateful to God for The Church at Brook Hills, a faith family who eagerly opened their Bibles every week not only to hear but also to obey the voice of God in Galatians for the glory of God among the nations.

David Platt

SERIES INTRODUCTION

Augustine said, "Where Scripture speaks, God speaks." The editors of the Christ-Centered Exposition Commentary series believe that where God speaks, the pastor must speak. God speaks through His written Word. We must speak from that Word. We believe the Bible is God breathed, authoritative, inerrant, sufficient, understandable, necessary, and timeless. We also affirm that the Bible is a Christ-centered book; that is, it contains a unified story of redemptive history of which Jesus is the hero. Because of this Christ-centered trajectory that runs from Genesis 1 through Revelation 22, we believe the Bible has a corresponding global-missions thrust. From beginning to end, we see God's mission as one of making worshipers of Christ from every tribe and tongue worked out through this redemptive drama in Scripture. To that end we must preach the Word.

In addition to these distinct convictions, the Christ-Centered Exposition Commentary series has some distinguishing characteristics. First, this series seeks to display exegetical accuracy. What the Bible says is what we want to say. While not every volume in the series will be a verse-by-verse commentary, we nevertheless desire to handle the text carefully and explain it rightly. Those who teach and preach bear the heavy responsibility of saying what God has said in His Word and declaring what God has done in Christ. We desire to handle God's Word faithfully, knowing that we must give an account for how we have fulfilled this holy calling (Jas 3:1).

Second, the Christ-Centered Exposition Commentary series has pastors in view. While we hope others will read this series, such as parents, teachers, small-group leaders, and student ministers, we desire to provide a commentary busy pastors will use for weekly preparation of biblically faithful and gospel-saturated sermons. This series is not academic in nature. Our aim is to present a readable and pastoral style of commentaries. We believe this aim will serve the church of the Lord Jesus Christ.

Third, we want the Christ-Centered Exposition Commentary series to be known for the inclusion of helpful illustrations and theologically driven applications. Many commentaries offer no help in illustrations, and few offer any kind of help in application. Often those that do offer illustrative material and application unfortunately give little serious attention to the text. While giving ourselves primarily to explanation, we also hope to serve readers by providing inspiring and illuminating illustrations coupled with timely and timeless application.

Finally, as the name suggests, the editors seek to exalt Jesus from every book of the Bible. In saying this, we are not commending wild allegory or fanciful typology. We certainly believe we must be constrained to the meaning intended by the divine Author Himself, the Holy Spirit of God. However, we also believe the Bible has a messianic focus, and our hope is that the individual authors will exalt Christ from particular texts. Luke 24:25-27,44-47; and John 5:39,46 inform both our hermeneutics and our homiletics. Not every author will do this the same way or have the same degree of Christ-centered emphasis. That is fine with us. We believe faithful exposition that is Christ centered is not monolithic. We do believe, however, that we must read the whole Bible as Christian Scripture. Therefore, our aim is both to honor the historical particularity of each biblical passage and to highlight its intrinsic connection to the Redeemer.

The editors are indebted to the contributors of each volume. The reader will detect a unique style from each writer, and we celebrate these unique gifts and traits. While distinctive in their approaches, the authors share a common characteristic in that they are pastoral theologians. They love the church, and they regularly preach and teach God's Word to God's people. Further, many of these contributors are younger voices. We think these new, fresh voices can serve the church well, especially among a rising generation that has the task of proclaiming the Word of Christ and the Christ of the Word to the lost world.

We hope and pray this series will serve the body of Christ well in these ways until our Savior returns in glory. If it does, we will have succeeded in our assignment.

David Platt
Daniel L. Akin
Tony Merida
Series Editors
February 2013

Galatians

Freed by Grace

GALATIANS 1:1-5

Main Idea: We cannot earn God's favor through legalism, for the gospel is free and freeing.

I. **Legalism Defined**
    A. Working in our own power
    B. Working according to our own rules
    C. Working to earn God's favor
II. **Legalism Destroyed**
    A. The gospel is free.
        1. God the Father has initiated our salvation.
        2. God the Son has accomplished our salvation.
    B. The gospel is freeing.
        1. By His grace, we are free from sin in this world.
        2. By His grace, we are free to share with this world.

India is known as a land of a million gods, multiplied millions, in fact. There are gods everywhere: cab drivers have gods on their dashboards, the streets are lined with religious vending stands, and people even worship trees on the sidewalk, bowing down and praying to them. I recently had the privilege of seeing this firsthand with a missions team from my own church. Suffice it to say, the people of India are extremely religious, working tirelessly for a right standing with God; nevertheless, peace remains elusive.

While the concept of grace, of God making peace with us (and not the other way around), is completely foreign to most people in India, it is also a foreign concept in many of the churches in our own culture. The very idea of God's unmerited favor is unique, revolutionary, and life transforming. In reality, every human being struggles to grasp the biblical truth of God's grace.

Everyone is born with a nature that insists that we can make our own way to God. Even after we are saved—saved by grace—there are still traces of a performance mentality that we all struggle with. We think we can earn God's favor by what we do. This ingrained mind-set of works-righteousness means that we have to be careful not to misinterpret passages that talk about obedience and discipleship. It is all too easy to lose sight of the grace that's at the heart of our faith. The hard sayings of Jesus can prompt us to ask, "What about grace?" That's an important question because if we leave grace behind, we become like every other religion in the world. We lose that which is distinct and eternally life transforming in the gospel, and we lose the very message that we are called to proclaim. In short, we lose our faith. Here are the apostle Paul's sobering words for anyone who preaches anything other than the true gospel of grace: "If anyone preaches to you a gospel contrary to what you received, a curse be on him!" (1:9). Eternal condemnation awaits those who preach contrary to the gracious gospel of Jesus Christ.

Galatians is a book that was written specifically to counter legalism and to address the centrality of grace in the church. As we study this book, we should begin to see more clearly what grace is, to be saturated with it, and to know when it is being taught accurately. When we hear a false gospel, we should be discerning enough to recognize it. This is exactly what the Galatian church, a new church that was just beginning to grow, was in danger of missing.

Whenever God is moving in a powerful way in the church, the adversary will always work to interject doubts, discord, and division, so we must be on guard. As God takes us to deeper and deeper places of abandonment to Him and His cause, we must be diligent to keep grace at the center of everything, even of radical obedience. We must be on guard against anything that would compromise the core of grace that makes the gospel worth celebrating and sharing. Galatians gives us a picture of grace that is both good and glorious.

Galatians was most likely written to young churches that Paul had planted during his first missionary journey. (There is considerable debate over the recipients and date of this letter. For a good discussion on these issues, see Schreiner, *Galatians*, 22–31.) The apostle's introduction in verses 1-5 sets the tone for the first chapter, and beyond that, for the entire book. This book is addressed to churches in Galatia, likely churches that were just beginning to grow. The most important background information deals with a group of people called the Judaizers who had infiltrated the church. These false teachers were saying that in order to be saved, you had to believe in Christ *plus* you had to basically become a Jew. In other words, you had to follow the laws of the Old Testament and, most notably, you had to be circumcised. This issue of circumcision is precisely what the Jerusalem Council had to address in Acts 15.

In Acts 15:1 Luke tells us the issue being discussed: "Some men came down from Judea and began to teach the brothers: 'Unless you are circumcised according to the custom prescribed by Moses, you cannot be saved!'" Gentiles in Jerusalem were coming to faith in Christ, but a group of Jews were saying that in order for them to be accepted in the church (i.e., in order for them to be Christians), these Gentiles needed to be circumcised. This was a huge moment in the early church because this issue was going to decide whether the gospel would stay pure or the church would adopt additives, so to speak, that would nullify grace. Thankfully, the church declared that circumcision was not necessary for salvation, so that at the end of the chapter, the council sent Paul and Barnabas along with several other men to share this news with the Gentile churches (Acts 15:22). It was good news for the churches, welcomed warmly (Acts 15:31). But even more importantly, for the sake of the gospel, the purity of grace was maintained in the body of Christ.

While commentators disagree over whether Galatians was written before or after the Jerusalem Council took place, it is clear that Paul directly confronted Judaizers—legalists, so to speak—who were attempting to invade the church in Galatia. They were "troubling" the church (Gal 1:7), throwing believers into confusion and perverting the gospel. So what does this first-century challenge have to do with us today? After all, we don't have a group of Judaizers spreading their message in our culture, and thankfully we don't have a lot of discussions about circumcision or some of the other Old Testament laws. Nevertheless, there will always be threats to the purity of the gospel, so we must guard against these in the church. Legalism is one threat that continually reemerges in different forms. Based on this picture of Judaizers in Galatians, we need to define this term *legalism*.

Legalism Defined

Working in Our Own Power

Spotting legalism and diagnosing it correctly is important because sometimes we label things as legalistic that are not legalistic. So what is legalism? Consider three different aspects of this term. First, it's working in our own power. Don't forget that Christ was prominent in the Judaizers' preaching, but it was Christ *plus* what man can bring to the table. Believe in Christ, they said, and then give your natural ability to obey the laws and rituals in the Old Testament. A contemporary form of this error is the idea that we're saved by grace, and then we live the Christian life in our own strength, essentially leaving grace behind. That's legalistic because it involves working in your own power.

Working According to Our Own Rules

Second, legalism is working according to our own rules. It involves adding rules beyond what God has already defined as the basis for His relationship with us. The New Testament is filled with commands from Christ for our eternal good. We don't need to add to them. Even today there are countless ways in which we come up with additional rules beyond what we have in the New Testament as the standard for our faith in Christ and our walk with Christ.

Working to Earn God's Favor

In addition to working in our own power and according to our own rules, the third aspect of legalism has to do with working to earn God's favor. Sometimes legalism is practiced in order to please men, but the main idea is that by doing certain things one increases in favor before God. This is where performance-based faith comes alive. The Judaizers taught that obedience to God's law was the way to ensure a right standing before God. Consequently, you enhance your spiritual standing before God based on what you do. This mind-set is prevalent today, and we are all prone to fall into it. We think, *If I'm reading the Bible, praying, going to worship, and doing a number of other good things, then I have favor before God.* But when we miss days in prayer or time in the Word, or if we don't attend worship, then we can start to think that God is not pleased with us. The startling truth of Christianity is that God's pleasure is not based on our performance. The legalist in us resists this, and we think, *Well, certainly I have to do* something. That may well be what made the Judaizers' heresy so appealing to the Galatian Christians. And it's why Paul charged them with deserting the gospel (1:6). He says anyone who preaches that God's favor is based on performance should, according to verses 8-9, be "anathema"—cursed, condemned. Whether it's Paul who preaches another gospel, or even an angel from heaven, he is to be damned (1:8). Needless to say, it is very serious to misrepresent the gospel.

Galatians was Martin Luther's favorite book. Luther was the father, so to speak, of the Reformation, and he lived at a time when all kinds of rules and regulations had been added to the gospel. You had to believe in Christ *plus* do certain things in order to be saved. Working in your own power according to the church's rules would help you earn righteousness before God. But Luther, like Paul, was stubborn and hard-headed when it came to the truth of the gospel. He said,

> Wherefore, God assisting me, my forehead shall be more hard than all men's foreheads. . . . Yea, I am glad even with all my heart, in this point to seem rebellious and obstinate. And here I confess that I am, and ever will be stout and stern, and will not one inch give place to any creature. (Luther, *Commentary*, 212)

Luther also said,

> Let this be then the conclusion of all together, that we will suffer our goods to be taken away, our name, our life, and all that we have: but the Gospel, our faith, Jesus Christ, we will never suffer to be wrested from us. . . . [L]et every Christian man here be proud and spare not, except he will deny Christ. (ibid.)

Luther's courage and conviction should inspire all of us. The gospel must be zealously defended, which means that legalism must be vehemently attacked and destroyed. So how does Paul do it? And how do we do it? How do we counter the thinking so ingrained in us that God's pleasure is based on our performance? I believe Galatians 1 gives us the answer. Below we'll look at two fundamental, life-changing truths that destroy legalism.

Legalism Destroyed

The first truth from Galatians 1 that destroys legalism is this:

The Gospel Is Free

Listen to how Paul starts this letter: "Grace to you and peace" (v. 3). This was a uniquely Christian greeting—"Grace to you"—and Paul starts and ends this letter with it. His final words are, "Brothers, the grace of our Lord Jesus Christ be with your spirit. Amen" (6:18). The term "grace" appears throughout Galatians (cf. seven times: 1:3,6,15; 2:9,21;

5:4; 6:18), and it's one of Paul's favorite words throughout his writings. He uses it 100 times in the New Testament, almost twice as many times as all the other New Testament writers combined (Morris, *Galatians*, 35). From the very beginning of this letter, Paul teaches us that God's favor is free. His salvation is free. His love, His mercy, His provision is free. It's not based on your performance; rather, it's based on *His* performance. Consider how this plays out through the work of God the Father and God the Son.

God the Father has initiated our salvation. The opening greeting speaks to this in verses 3-4: "Grace to you and peace from *God the Father*. . . . according to the will of *our God and Father*" (emphasis added). Grace is from God. The gospel is from God. It is God's will that His people would know His grace; He's designed it this way. Later, when Paul talks about how he came to faith in Christ, he describes his pre-conversion life this way:

> For you have heard about my former way of life in Judaism: I
> persecuted God's church to an extreme degree and tried to destroy it. I
> advanced in Judaism beyond many contemporaries among my people,
> because I was extremely zealous for the traditions of my ancestors.
> (1:13-14)

Notice the subject in these sentences: "I." But then there's a shift in the subject:

> But when God, who from my birth set me apart and called me by His
> grace, was pleased to reveal His Son in me, so that I could preach
> Him among the Gentiles, I did not immediately consult with anyone.
> (1:15)

Paul acknowledges that all his raging fanaticism was no match for the good pleasure of God. God set him apart, God called him, and God saved him by revealing Christ. And it was all by grace. You and I may not have the same background as Paul, but every follower of Christ has this same testimony. In the words of Ephesians,

> For He chose us in Him, before the foundation of the world, to be holy
> and blameless in His sight. In love He predestined us to be adopted
> through Jesus Christ for Himself, according to His favor and will, to
> the praise of His glorious grace. (Eph 1:4-6)

Praise God, it is the Father's will to show us grace, not our will. That's what Paul says: "So then it does not depend on human will or effort but on God who shows mercy" (Rom 9:16). Paul didn't deserve mercy; he didn't even ask for it. It pursued him. The same holds true for us: we do not deserve mercy, nor do we even know how to seek it. It seeks us. And it finds us. Mercy comes running, and by His grace, God pursues you with His love. His pleasure in you is not dependent on your pursuit of Him, but His pursuit of you. That's one of the reasons the Judaizers were criticizing the gospel of free grace that Paul was preaching and trying to discredit his ministry.

Paul's reaction to the criticisms of the Judaizers was twofold. First, in Galatians 1 and in the beginning of Galatians 2 he tells them that the gospel is not invented by man.

Paul essentially says, "I didn't make this up." He gives specific details about his time in Arabia, a short trip he made to Jerusalem, and the time he spent in Syria and Cilicia (1:17-21), and his whole point is to show that he didn't learn this gospel from any other man. As an apostle, he learned this gospel directly from Christ, and this gospel was identical to the gospel that had been revealed to the other apostles who had lived and walked with Jesus.

There's a second aspect to Paul's reaction to the Judaizers, and it's the flip side of his previous claim that the gospel was not invented by man. The gospel is revealed by God; there is nothing man-made about it. The good news is that God became a man and lived a perfect life that He might die on the cross for our sins and be raised from the dead in victory over sin so that all who believe in Him will be saved, not based on anything they have done, but based solely on what He has done. This gospel goes against every single strain of pride that dominates our hearts, which indicates that it had to come from God. He initiates our salvation, which is why Paul says that abandoning the gospel of free grace is an abandonment of God Himself. That would be a deadly error.

So far we've seen the work of the Father in initiating our salvation. But there's another, complementary aspect to this.

God the Son has accomplished our salvation. Grace and peace come not only from God the Father in verse 3, but also from "our Lord Jesus Christ." The Father and the Son are closely identified in the work of salvation. The Son is the One "who gave Himself for our sins to rescue us from this present evil age" (v. 4). This is the core truth of the gospel. Salvation is not about what man can do; salvation is about what Christ has already done, and He has done everything necessary for our salvation. Paul says that He, Jesus, gave Himself "for" our sins. This word "for" is important, and Paul uses it again in 2:20 and 3:13. The apostle speaks of Jesus giving His life in the place of sinners who deserve God's judgment (ibid., 37). He has paid our sin debt.

God's pleasure is not based on our performance, but on the performance of Christ, who gave Himself for our sins. The only way we can be accepted before God is through Christ. Yet, these churches in Galatia were missing the significance of the death of Christ by adding other qualifications. That's why Paul says, rather forcefully, that we malign the gospel when we add to grace, which is precisely what the Judaizers were doing.

Don't forget, however, that much of the teaching of the Judaizers was right down the line, biblically speaking. They acknowledged Jesus as the Messiah, and they even acknowledged His death on the cross. They claimed to believe all the truths that other Christians believed, and they certainly weren't telling people that they denied the gospel. Instead, they were improving it, adding requirements and standards from the old covenant to the new covenant. But the reality is that as soon as you add anything to grace, you lose grace altogether. There's no middle ground.

Think about it: If you were about to drink a glass of clean water, and then someone added a drop of poison to it, would you still drink it? It's close to pure, right? No, it's *totally* contaminated and undrinkable as soon as that drop of poison hits the water. It's the same way with the gospel. If you tamper with and add anything to grace, you lose the whole gospel. This is why Paul opposes adding human work to the work of Christ for salvation. The gospel does not tell us what we have to do to please God; instead, it announces that God is pleased with us based solely on Christ's accomplishment in His death and resurrection and our identification with Him. We don't need Christ plus this or Christ plus that. We need Christ, period.

Peace can only come in Christ, and we need to be confident in this. So many times we believe God loves us, but secretly we think that His love depends on how we're doing in the Christian life. But remember, God is pleased with you, not based on your performance, but based on the work of Christ for you. This same Christ now lives in you, and even your good works are the result of His power and presence within you.

Not only do we malign the gospel when we add to grace, but **we misunderstand the gospel when we cheapen grace**. One of the accusations that always accompanies the free gospel of grace is, "Doesn't that mean people can just live however they want?" (See Rom 6:15.) This is one of the dangers or risks of grace, namely, that some people will abuse grace and take it to mean that this free gift gives them license and freedom to live however they want. Paul addresses this error more specifically later in Galatians 5:13, but suffice it to say at this point, this is a misunderstanding of grace. First, grace is not cheap. The cost of grace is a cross, where Jesus gave Himself for our sins. Second, grace changes our lives. You can't have this free grace without it changing your life. In 2:14 Paul confronts Peter and the believers with him for "deviating from the truth of the gospel" by their hypocritical actions. Their actions were contradicting the grace they believed and proclaimed. Grace brings about change.

If we're honest, different parts of the Bible can almost sound like different gospels. For instance, Jesus said, "Go, sell your belongings and give to the poor, and you will have treasure in heaven" (Matt 19:21). That sounds very different from what Paul says in Galatians. In fact, if Jesus hadn't been the One to say it, we'd wonder if that was legalism! Or consider Jesus' words:

> But everyone who hears these words of Mine and doesn't act on them will be like a foolish man who built his house on the sand. The rain fell, the rivers rose, the winds blew and pounded that house, and it collapsed. And its collapse was great! (Matt 7:26-27)

This is where you can get into a lot of trouble quoting Jesus in the church! The relationship between Paul and James can also be difficult to understand at times. Paul says that we are justified by faith alone (Rom 3:28), and yet James asks, "Are you willing to learn that faith without works is useless?" (Jas 2:20). This is one of the reasons Luther, who loved Galatians, used to say that he wanted to throw "Jimmy" into the stove.

So which is it? Do we side with Jesus and James, or is Paul right? Before you answer, consider that even Paul confuses us. We're used to hearing about free grace in Galatians and in verses like "For you are saved by grace through faith" (Eph 2:8), but then we hear Paul talk about Christ's second coming as a time when He [Jesus] will be "taking vengeance with flaming fire on those who don't know God and on those who don't obey the gospel of our Lord Jesus" (2 Thess 1:8). If we didn't know any better, we'd call Paul a legalist.

The solution to this dilemma is to understand that throughout the New Testament, there is one gospel. So the truth doesn't change, but different books address different audiences. In Galatians Paul writes to people who were trying to add to the gospel. James, on the other hand, was writing to people who were trying to take away from the gospel and cheapen it by downplaying obedience in Christ. Nevertheless, it's all one gospel, and we must be careful not to malign it, nor to misunderstand it.

Rather than maligning or misunderstanding the gospel, we need to marvel at it, and **we marvel at the gospel when we trust in grace.** The key word here is "trust," sometimes translated as "faith." We must believe that the gospel is free. God the Father has initiated our salvation, and God the Son has accomplished our salvation, wholly apart from anything we have done or would ever be able to do. That's why the gospel is called "good news." Such grace extended to unworthy sinners is worth our marveling.

The Gospel Is Freeing

Earlier we noted that there are two truths that destroy legalism. The first truth is that the gospel is free, which Paul is zealous to make clear. Second, the gospel is freeing. In verse 4 Paul says that Jesus gave Himself for our sins, "to rescue us from this present evil age." This word "rescue" is used in Acts to talk about how the Israelites were rescued, or freed, from slavery (Acts 7:34). It's also used to describe how Peter was rescued, or freed, from prison (Acts 12:11) and how Paul was rescued by Claudius from being lynched by a mob (Acts 23:27). The word "rescue" in Galatians 1:4 speaks not simply of being delivered from the guilt of our sin, though that is certainly true, but also of being delivered from a power—the power of this present evil age. "This present evil age" refers to the world we live in and all of its ways. Now obviously we still live in this world, but there is a sense in which we've been taken out of it. We no longer have to live like this world, pursuing what this world pursues, loving what this world loves, indulging in what this world indulges in. We're free!

The Judaizers were accusing Paul of preaching a gospel that led to loose living. Because they stressed the Old Testament law and morality, they thought that taking the law away would lead to lawless living and license to sin. In Galatians 5 Paul explains why this isn't the case.

We're not freed into nothingness; rather, we are freed into Christ, who changes us by His Spirit from the inside out. We are freed to live based on Christ's power at work in us. Don't miss the point: our obedience is not legalistic. We're not working in our own power according to our own rules to earn God's favor. No, we're working in His power according to His rules and we know we have His favor, not based on what we do, but based on all that Christ has done for us! The gospel frees us to live as we were created to live—in Christ!

By His grace, we are free from sin in this world. We are saved from the evil age we live in and all of its sinful attitudes, values, and actions. Whether its Jesus' costly calls in the Gospels or the commands in Paul's letters, we don't walk away saying, "Legalistic!" Because Christ lives in us, and because He empowers us by His Spirit, we are free to obey His Word.

By His grace, we are free to share with this world. Paul says, "To whom be the glory forever and ever. Amen" (1:5). God gives us His free grace for His glory. Paul makes a related point:

> But when God, who from my birth set me apart and called me by His grace, was pleased to reveal His Son in me, so that I could preach Him among the Gentiles, I did not immediately consult with anyone. (1:15-16)

Why did God give Paul such grace? So that Paul would preach the gospel to the Gentiles. It was private revelation for public communication. This is the kind of grace that frees us to speak, to tell. But it's not just Paul who has been saved in order to proclaim the good news. Whether it's going to an unreached people group on the other side of the planet, or bearing witness to Christ in your workplace, you and I have the privilege and the responsibility, as those who have received God's grace, to share this gospel with everyone. Grace frees us to pass along this good news.

Reflect and Discuss

1. Explain the following statement: Everyone has legalistic tendencies. Give some examples of how legalism shows up in your own thoughts and actions.
2. How does legalism undermine the gospel?
3. What's the difference between legalism and zealous obedience?
4. Why is it important to be clear about the origin of the gospel, whether from God or from man?

5. Why is the fact that the Father initiated salvation important for understanding that the gospel is free?
6. In what ways do we add to the gospel? What are some "Jesus + something else" messages taught today?
7. What does Paul say about those who preach false gospels? Do you think Paul is out of control in this passage? Why or why not?
8. Does free grace lead to carelessness about sin? Explain.
9. How do Paul's words about pleasing Christ, not men, affect you? Do you struggle with the desire to please others over Christ? How might we fight this sin?
10. What practical steps can you take to avoid legalism as you share the gospel with unbelievers?

Contending for the Gospel

GALATIANS 1:6-10

Main Idea: Amazed by the Galatian believers' turn from the gospel of Christ, Paul explains why such a decision is problematic.

I. **The Galatians' Departure (1:6-7a)**
   A. The nature of turning from the gospel
   B. What we learn about the gospel
II. **The False Teachers' Distortion (1:7b)**
III. **The Universal Warning (1:8-9)**
IV. **The Apostle's Ambition (1:10)**

In this passage Paul is addressing the problem in Galatia: false teachers are spreading a false gospel. And to make matters worse, the Galatians are listening to them!

The Bible deals further with the subject of false teaching and false gospels in the book of Jude. There Jude urges believers to "contend for the faith" (v. 3). The word translated "contend" was an athletic term, meaning to "agonize greatly" or "struggle." Indeed, contending for the gospel is like participating in an agonizing athletic contest, and that is why many do not contend. But all Christians, not just the clergy, are called to be such athletes. Each of us must be ready to give "a reason for the hope that is in [us]" (1 Pet 3:15).

To whom do you talk about the gospel? To your co-workers? Your teammates? Some friends at a restaurant or coffee shop? In our interactions with others, we should always be contending for the gospel—that is, giving a defense of what we believe about Christ. We will, however, all meet challengers as we do. For Paul, the challengers were known as the Judaizers.

Contending is a relevant subject not only for spurring us on to greater witness, but also for reminding us of the importance of knowing what we believe. Many high school graduates go off to college and soon consider abandoning the Christian faith on which they were raised. Why? Among a host of contributing factors is the fact that they simply were never prepared to contend for the faith. As a result, a skeptical professor, a group of unbelieving friends, or an unbelieving boyfriend or girlfriend may cause them to doubt the faith altogether—or at least to question its importance to daily life. This trend is a good reminder that every believer must be rooted in the essentials of the faith early on in his or her Christian journey.

Unprepared students make me think of the *Rocky* film series. In the third movie Rocky Balboa is steamrolling his handpicked opponents, but then he meets "Clubber" Lang, played by Mr. T. Lang is a real challenger, so Apollo Creed decides to train Rocky; his training program is essential if Rocky is to beat such an opponent. Likewise, Christian students must receive theological training before they take a class from that skeptical professor or encounter those persuasive students with worldviews contrary to theirs. If not, their own "Clubber" Langs just might knock them out.

In Galatians 1 Paul is training his audience to contend with their spiritual opponents by showing his hearers how to detect false gospels and recognize the true one. Similarly, good pastors, teachers, and parents will train students to contend for the faith. While we do not train them to knock out their challengers physically, we do want them able to "knock out" arguments and strongholds. In doing so they may ultimately win a person, not just an argument (2 Tim 2:25).

This letter should give all believers "eye of the tiger" inspiration to contend for the gospel of Christ. Maybe your challenger is a friend, whom you love, but he or she does not understand why you insist that Jesus is the only way to God and thinks you are a narrow-minded Bible-thumper. Maybe your challenger is a rebellious teen turning away from God and the church, claiming, "It's all a myth." Maybe you have a co-worker who is reading the works of Daniel Dennett and Christopher Hitchens and is buying into the new atheist movement, slowly losing all respect for your beliefs. Perhaps a friend at the coffee shop, who just wants to talk about UFOs, challenges you! Maybe you are facing a difficult challenge in trying to explain grace to a religious Pharisee. In any case, allow Galatians 1:6-10 to encourage and educate you.

The Galatians' Departure
GALATIANS 1:6-7A

The proper way to begin a letter in Roman times was with thanksgiving. Here, however, because Paul is so burdened by the Galatians' error, he offers none. Instead, he is like a parent who sees his kid running into the road and yells, "Hey, there's a car coming! Watch out!" He offers no pious platitudes, only passionate warning.

Paul would not have received an "A" in Quintilian's literature class. Quintilian (AD 35–95) was the day's expert in classical style and rhetoric. He said a man should not "open in such a wild and exclamatory nature"; instead, a sane man would employ "a courteous and natural opening" (*Institutio,* 509). Paul does indeed open with a wild, exclamatory nature: "I am amazed!" He does so because of the serious nature of the problem. He was not amazed that there were false teachers; he was amazed by the Galatian Christians' interest in them!

The Nature of Turning from the Gospel

Notice in this passage the nature of their "turning" and what we learn about the gospel itself.

Their turning away from the gospel was serious! The Galatians were in the process of switching teams. John Stott notes that the word *turning* means "to transfer one's allegiance." It was used of soldiers in the army who would go fight for the other side, or of politicians who would transfer to the other political party (*Message of Galatians,* 21). Can you imagine a Cowboys fan wearing a Redskins shirt, or a Red Sox fan wearing a Yankees cap? That is serious turning. In my world, it is amazing to think that Rick Pitino, former coach of the University of Kentucky, now coaches Louisville. But at an infinitely more important level, it is an amazing thing for Paul to think that the Galatians, who had heard the truth of the gospel, were putting on a different jersey. The Galatians had come to Christ and put on the robes of righteousness and were now trying to turn back to the trash can to retrieve their old clothes of works-based religion.

The Galatians' transfer hurt Paul because he saw them as his spiritual children. He later said to them, "My children, I am again suffering labor pains for you until Christ is formed in you" (4:19). He was in agony, desiring to see them grow into Christlikeness and knowing that their turning was anything but an insignificant event. His passion reminds us that truth should matter to us! When someone is turning away from Christ, it should grieve us. And when someone is walking in the gospel of grace, it should thrill us. John writes, "I have no greater joy than this: to hear that my children are walking in the truth" (3 John 4).

One day a parent came to my office. She was totally broken because her daughter was dating a Mormon and was unable to distinguish the great differences between Christianity and Mormonism. She grieved to see her child turning to a false gospel because she knew that nothing is more important than the true gospel (cf. 1 Cor 15:3-4). Nothing should be more important to us.

Their turning away from the gospel happened so soon! Paul is "amazed" that those in the churches at Galatia were turning "so quickly!" The words "so quickly" call to mind the golden calf incident in Exodus 32:7-8. Israel had just been liberated from Egypt, received God's law, and made a covenant with God. But immediately—while Moses was up on the mountain speaking with the Lord—they made a golden calf and worshiped that idol in the place of their Redeemer. Amazing!

Put yourself in Paul's sandals. You go out to start these churches through many personal tribulations. You travel over mountains, face danger, and are left for dead before you see some people coming to Christ and churches forming as a result. But then, immediately after these churches are established, you hear that those new believers are turning away from the faith. How would you respond?

Imagine you just spent three years ministering to an unreached city in East Asia. Not long before you went home on furlough, you began to see the first converts among a people group there. You have just heard that the believers you left behind are now blending pagan worship with the gospel. How would you respond? Are you amazed? Astonished? Shocked? Dismayed? Angry?

You can hear Paul's anguish in this letter as he says things like, "Christ has liberated us to be free. Stand firm then and don't submit again to a yoke of slavery" (5:1). You can hear his frustration in verse 3 of chapter 1: "You foolish Galatians! Who has hypnotized you?" How quickly new believers can drift away from the grace of God into false teaching!

Their turning away was not hopeless. The situation of the Christians in Galatia was desperate but not beyond hope. The word translated "turning" is a continuous present tense verb, which means that they were in the process. Even though one might make too much of this, Schreiner states that the context as a whole indicates that it was a process (*Galatians*, 84n4). The good news was that through faithful contending for the gospel, Paul could correct them.

This idea of correction reminds me of the mother I mentioned earlier. She kept agonizing over her daughter, correcting her until she came to embrace the truth of the gospel, too. Later in the book Paul tells the Galatians not to "give up" (6:9). He encourages them and challenges them to consider where they went wrong: "You were running well. Who prevented you from obeying the truth?" (5:7). As long as our drifting friends are still breathing, let us not stop contending for the faith.

What We Learn about the Gospel

Three important truths accompany a person's tragic turn from the gospel.

When you turn from the gospel, you turn from God Himself (v. 6). Paul says that the Galatians are turning away from "Him," not merely from a set of principles. When you turn from the gospel, you are turning from the God of all grace. You are turning from the Christ "who gave Himself for our sins to rescue us from this present evil age" (v. 4). Paul says he is amazed that the Galatians are turning from their Redeemer, the fountain of all grace.

Today you might hear something like this: "I believe in Jesus, but I have no interest in the Bible." Statements such as that one reveal that many want to hold on to God but abandon the gospel. They want to know God, but they don't accept the idea of Him punishing His Son in our place. That dismissive approach will not work. When you turn from the gospel, you turn from God Himself.

Disbelieving the gospel is no small error. In fact, it tops Bill Buckner's infamous miss. Buckner was a famous first basemen for the Red Sox. He was known for a successful career until he allowed a ground ball to go between his legs in game six of the 1986 World Series. It led to his team's loss that day as well as to the eventual loss of the whole series to the Mets. Do not let the gospel slip by you: grab hold of it in its entirety. If you miss Christ, you will lose everything.

When you turn from the gospel, you turn from the grace of Christ (v. 6). "The grace of Christ" is a synonym for the gospel (cf. 5:4). Remember, the Judaizers believed salvation was Jesus + circumcision and the requirements of the OT law. But salvation is not Jesus + anything. Why? Because salvation is by grace alone through faith in Christ alone. Paul is reminding his children of that message. Any other messenger, Christians should note, plays for the other team. The other team could be labeled "human achievement," since the other religions of the world all share a works-based salvation system. Paul represented the "divine accomplishment" team, who believed Christ has already accomplished the work for us and offers us salvation by His grace.

Notice how the words "called" and "grace" are together both here and in verse 15. The Galatians were called *by* grace, and they were called *into* the realm of grace. This type of *call* denotes God's sovereign action and believers' experience. When God calls you to Christ, you sense His power. You sense God dealing with you. Just as He called Abraham, Moses, and Paul, He calls sinners to Himself today. He calls us not because of any good in us but because of His grace.

Turning from the gospel is like stepping onto a performance-religion treadmill. Do you like treadmills? I don't. I do not enjoy running for three miles only to end up exhausted and in the same place 30 minutes later! Works-based religion is a system that gets you nowhere and only leaves you worn out. While works certainly matter, we should note they are the *result* of true faith, not the *basis* for it.

When you turn from the gospel, you have nowhere else to go (vv. 6-7). Paul tells the Galatians that they are "turning to a *different* gospel," but adds, "not that there is *another* gospel" (emphasis added). In other words, Paul says the false teachers' message is no gospel at all. There is only one gospel. Paul seems to choose his words carefully to make this point. In verse 6 he uses the word translated "different," the Greek word is *heteros*. It means "another of a *different* nature." (We get terms like *heterosexual* from this word.) A biblical example of this concept is in Hebrews 7:11, where it is used to explain that a different kind of priest—not one from the order of Aaron—is needed, namely, Christ. The Galatians were turning to a hetero-gospel, a gospel of a different nature. But in verse 7 Paul uses the Greek word *allos*, translated "another," which means "another of the *same* nature." He says there is not an *allos* gospel. A biblical example is in John chapters 14–16 regarding the Holy Spirit. When Jesus leaves, another of the same kind *(allos)* will come (John 14:16). We might have another cup of the same kind of coffee, but we cannot have another of the same kind of gospel (George, *Galatians*, 93). There is only one gospel.

In all likelihood the false teachers were saying that their gospel was not different from what Paul taught. But Paul says, "Yes, it is." There is nothing else like the gospel of Christ. Unfortunately, false teachers have been using the same "Oh, we believe in Jesus, too" line for centuries.

But when you go deeper into the teachings of any cult, you realize that it presents a hetero-gospel (cf. 2 Cor 11:3-4).

The point is that there is no other way to be right with God, to experience forgiveness of sin, apart from the gospel of Christ Jesus (see John 14:6-7). It is difficult for people to embrace the exclusiveness of the gospel when they swim in a sea of religious pluralism and philosophical relativism. We often hear, "All religions are equally valid, and there is no one truth." But finding right relationship with God is not like selecting a deodorant. You may choose any of a number of antiperspirants to keep you fresh, but that is not the case when it comes to securing eternal life. Only one path to God will do: Jesus. He has no equal. He is not one among many religious leaders. He is the one and only Messiah.

Perhaps you think this discussion is purely an apologetic conversation devoid of much meaning for your local church. I would beg to differ. One of my friends who is a pastor surveyed his church body regarding some doctrinal questions. He pastors in the Bible Belt, serving among people who have grown up attending worship services. To his shock, he found that 78 percent of the respondents in his church believed that it is possible to go to heaven apart from believing in Christ. Now, while this was not a scientific survey of all churches and was only the experience of one pastor surveying his congregation, the results should make you wonder what you would find in your congregation were the same study given there. Do people think there is only one gospel? If you feel, as I do, that my friend's findings are probably in line with what others would find elsewhere, then the need to contend for the true gospel *within* the church is glaringly obvious.

The False Teachers' Distortion
GALATIANS 1:7B

How do you detect false teachers? Consider two truths about false teachers in verse 7.

False teachers create confusion and division. Paul says, "There are some who are *troubling* you" (emphasis added). The word *trouble* means to "shake" or "agitate" or "throw into confusion" (George, *Galatians*, 94). The Galatians' minds were like clothes dryers at the laundry mat. Have you seen the dryers with the glass fronts? I sometimes washed my own clothes when I was single, and I would sit there at the laundry mat and watch the clothes tumble, shake, rattle, and roll inside the drum. Likewise, the Galatians' thoughts were shaken and thrown into confusion as their minds tried to reconcile Paul's teachings with the new, false doctrines.

Consider another biblical example of the kind of teachers who threw the believers into perplexity. When in Acts 15 the apostles got together at the Jerusalem Council to discuss the Gentiles coming to faith in Christ, they had to deal with the false teachers who were insisting that the Gentiles be circumcised (Acts 15:1). After uniting in the doctrine of salvation through grace (15:11), they sent a letter to the Gentiles saying, "Some without our authorization went out from us and troubled you with their words and unsettled your hearts" (15:24). False teachers were "troubling" believers and "unsettling" them. That is the nature of false teachers who wish to distort the pure gospel of grace.

To distort the gospel is to destroy the church because the church is created and lives by the gospel. The greatest troublemakers in the church are those who wish to distort the gospel message. I believe Satan operates more effectively through false gospels than through any other avenue. He twists, confuses, and changes the gospel, using philosophy and rule-keeping to put people in mental manacles that blind their eyes to the truth.

Behind every false teacher is the ultimate false teacher, Satan, who lives to create confusion and to lock people in spiritual bondage (2 Tim 2:26). Just as he did in Galatia, the evil one encourages false teachers to creep in subtly like wolves. False teachers do not walk around and say, "Hug me, I'm a false apostle." They are not always readily recognizable, unlike the stereotypical overweight, bombastic, hypocritical preacher with a bad hairpiece in B-movies and television dramas—though undoubtedly there are many false teachers on television. Instead, false teachers appear perfectly benign. They may be pop icons, people in your school, or friendly faces you pass in the halls of your church. Anyone promoting something other than the gospel, thereby placing mental manacles on people, is rightly identified as a false teacher.

False teachers reverse the gospel. Paul says that they "change" or "pervert" or "distort" (ESV) the gospel. "It is a word denoting a radical change, like changing water into blood, fresh water into salt water, feasting into mourning, daylight into darkness" (Dunn in Schreiner, *Galatians*, 86). In fact, some have suggested that the better way to render this word is "reverse." Jerome said, "It means to set behind what is in front, and putting what is in front, behind" (in George, *Galatians*, 95). That is certainly appropriate because that's exactly what the false teachers were doing: they were distorting the gospel by reversing the gospel!

What do I mean by reversing the gospel? There is a particular order to the gospel message. It goes like this:

> *For you are saved by grace through faith, and this is not from yourselves; it is God's gift—not from works, so that no one can boast. For we are His creation, created in Christ Jesus for good works, which God prepared ahead of time so that we should walk in them.*
> (Eph 2:8-10)

Notice we are (1) saved by grace alone (2) for good works. We do not receive grace after we have worked for salvation. That would be the reversal of the gospel. If a person says, "I'm going to do enough good things to be right with God and merit His grace and be saved," then we must inform him that he has officially reversed the gospel. He has put what was in the back into the front. There is an order to the gospel. False teachers distort this message of hope.

How are people distorting the gospel today? That answer is simple. People teach, either through false religious systems or through myths common to our culture, that you merit eternal life by your goodness or your works. One such myth has been dubbed "moralistic therapeutic deism." Adherents believe that one simply needs to believe in a god, but not that such a god might be involved in a person's life (deism). They feel that one needs to "be good" (moralistic) in order to "feel good" (therapeutic). If a person can believe in a god and basically do good things, they rationalize, then surely that person will go to heaven. Understand that while such thinking may be popular, it does not reflect the gospel.

Some might object to that truth with a rebuttal like this one: "But my friend is a Buddhist, and he's a nice guy. He's a moral guy. His family is polite." I would respond by saying, "I'm not denying that. I'm not denying that people who follow other religions can be moral people. Here's what I do deny: that morality can get you to heaven." While morality can keep you out of jail, it cannot keep you out of hell. If morality could save you, then Jesus did not need to die.

You see, you need something far greater than morality: you need perfect righteousness. Only perfectly righteous people, not people who are merely moral, can go to heaven. And no one in history has been perfectly righteous except Jesus. We need His righteousness. We should not complain that there is only one way to heaven; we should marvel at the fact that there is a way. Stand in awe of the reality that despite our sin and rebellion God sent the God-man to save us. Only through Jesus—the way, the truth, and the life—can we experience saving grace.

"But those who follow a different religion are sincere," some would argue. "Shouldn't sincerity matter?" I would not say that people following false religions are not sincere, but I will point out the biblical truth that sincerity cannot save. There is such a thing as "zeal . . . not according to knowledge" (Rom 10:2). In sincerely trying to reach heaven through any path other than salvation through Jesus, a person disregards righteousness from God and attempts to establish his or her own. He or she fails to submit to God's righteousness (cf. Rom 10:3). Think of it this way: A racer may run fast but still fail to reach his destination because he was headed in the wrong direction! There is only one valid alternative to works-based righteousness, and that is trusting in Christ.

Any works-based system is a *hopeless* system because we are not merely supposed to be moral; we must be perfectly righteous. We know we cannot achieve this. Further, the ultimate goal of Christianity is not morality; it is union with Christ. Works-based systems are also *despairing* because one can never know if he or she has done enough good works to measure up. Worse, they are *Christ-less* in that they deny that Jesus' work on the cross is sufficient or, in some cases, necessary. Finally, works based-systems are *man-centered*; they glorify humans, not God.

What is the alternative to works-based systems? Christ's righteousness given to us by grace alone through faith alone.

The Universal Warning
GALATIANS 1:8-9

Paul expresses his anger toward false teachers in verses 8-9. He pronounces a curse on anyone who proclaims a counterfeit gospel. He says it twice for emphasis and probably to clarify that he didn't lose his mind in verse 8:

> But even if we or an angel from heaven should preach to you a gospel other than what we have preached to you, a curse be on him! As we have said before, I now say again: If anyone preaches to you a gospel contrary to what you received, a curse be on him! (Gal 1:8-9)

What are we to make of this "curse"? The curse reminds us of the sobering responsibility we have as Christian teachers. Observe how Paul says that "if anyone" preaches a false gospel, a curse should be on that individual. He does not remove himself from this pronouncement, either. He says, "if we or an angel" preach another gospel. He essentially says, "If I start reversing this order, let me be cursed."

There are many false teachers, and as Paul told the Corinthians, "Satan disguises himself as an angel of light," manipulating and leading many away from pure devotion to Christ (2 Cor 11:13-15). Paul tells us in Galatians that a false teacher should not be deemed merely a heretic; he or she should be eternally condemned.

Someone might say, "But I like the way another religion makes me feel. It feels good to think I am earning favor with God through what I do." No one is denying you might feel something positive through pursuing another religion or by creating your own version of Christianity. But Satan is a *deceiver,* my friend; he can make anything feel good. I am reminded of the story of Simon the sorcerer recorded in Acts 8:9-25. His teaching felt so good to his hearers that some were calling him "the Great Power of God." But while he was "claiming to be somebody great" (v. 9) and the people were enjoying the astounding things he did, his message and his motive were fraudulent. He could only lead people astray.

Paul's warning reminds us not only of our holy responsibility as teachers, but also of the centrality of the gospel. This "curse" shows us that the gospel must remain the priority of Christian leaders. We must, therefore, ask this question about our church leaders: "Is he preaching the gospel?" That is the key question. In Philippians 1:12-18 Paul speaks about those preaching with bad motives; they taught out of envy and jealousy, but at least they were preaching Christ. What did he say about such teachers? He chose to rejoice because of them (Phil 1:18). He did so because his main concern was the purity of the message, not the motives of the messenger. The gospel alone saves.

The gospel is essential because **Christ's glory is at stake**. False gospels always glorify man because they boast in human achievements. The real gospel boasts only in the Lord (Gal 6:14). Spurgeon said, "If you meet with a system of theology which magnifies man, flee from it as far as you can" ("Non Nobis, Domine"). If we could be good enough and do enough and keep enough rules to merit eternal life, then we could sing about ourselves instead of Jesus. But that is not the case.

The gospel is also essential because **people's souls are at stake**. Paul knew this was no marginal issue; it was a momentous issue. In Romans 9:3 he says, "I could almost wish to be cursed and cut off from the Messiah for the benefit of my brothers." He said that he would rather be anathema than to see his brothers condemned. That is how seriously he took this matter. Jesus said it would be better for a man to have a millstone put around his neck and be cast into the sea than to cause someone else to stumble and disbelieve the truth of the gospel (Matt 18:6).

The gospel is also essential because **the health of the church is at stake**. Paul knew that the churches in Galatia were in their infancy. In Galatians 4:19 he tells them that he is in pain, laboring with them. He knows that if they miss the gospel, they miss everything. Here is what this means for us as a church: we can have disagreements over some things, but we must unite on the essentials of the gospel. There are open-handed issues and closed-handed issues; the gospel is the only closed-handed issue. I will die for the gospel, but not for a style of music, nor because I think one spiritual gift is better than another, nor over details about the end times, nor because I do not like tambourines in the worship service. Yet sadly, within many churches more people divide over issues not pertaining to the gospel than over this matter of first importance.

The Apostle's Ambition
GALATIANS 1:10

This verse is a transitional verse, linking the previous and coming sections. Paul expresses his ambition to please Christ, not men. He says, "For am I now trying to win the favor of people, or God? Or am I striving to please people?" Apparently some thought that Paul avoided preaching circumcision and the law as a requirement because he wanted to gain favor with the Gentiles. The next phrase, however, shows that he has no interest in pleasing people; his goal is pleasing God by preaching the true gospel.

Paul continues: "If I were still trying to please people, I would not be a slave of Christ." In other words, if Paul desired to be a people-pleaser, then he would never have turned his life over to Christ. He was formerly admired for his Pharisaical zeal. If his goal were admiration, then he would have remained a Pharisee. Jesus told the Pharisees,

"While accepting glory from one another, you don't seek the glory that comes from the only God" (John 5:44). Paul's goal was not to receive glory from people. His concern was for the glory of Christ, the health of the church, and the destiny of the souls of men and women.

If your goal in life is to be liked, then you will not be a faithful and fruitful Christian. I am not implying you should be a jerk. I am merely pointing out that followers of Jesus experience opposition. If people despised Jesus, some will despise you as His follower (see John 15:20; 2 Tim 3:12; 1 Pet 4:12-19; 1 John 3:13). You need to aspire to something greater than being cool. Aspire to being faithful.

Whom do you long to please? Whose approval matters most? Proverbs warns, "The fear of man is a snare" (Prov 29:25). The word *fear* often means to "reverence," to "stand in awe of," to "worship." Seeking the approval of people, then, is idolatry. In concerning yourself with what everyone else thinks about you, you are worshiping people, not God. The old hymn "I'd Rather Have Jesus" captures the right spirit:

I'd rather have Jesus than men's applause;
I'd rather be faithful to His dear cause;
I'd rather have Jesus than worldwide fame,
I'd rather be true to His holy name. (Rhea Miller, 1922)

This song reflects the spirit of our brother, Athanasius, a leader at the Council of Nicea in AD 325. He argued for the biblical Jesus at a time when doing so was not popular. People said, "Athanasius, the whole world is against you." To this he replied, "Then I'm against the whole world." So be it.

Are you a servant of Christ? Adore Him in your heart. Recognize the grace that He has given you and the death He endured for you. Contend for this message with courage and with the power of the Spirit that is yours in Christ.

Reflect and Discuss

1. Why must we contend for the gospel? What hinders people from contending?
2. What are some of the main arguments against Christianity today? How do you respond to them?
3. Are you having gospel conversations with people? Why or why not? Stop and pray for someone who needs to trust in Christ alone for salvation.

4. Why was Paul "amazed" by the Galatians? What might quickly "turning" away from devotion to God look like today?
5. Do you think Paul is out of control in this passage? Explain.
6. What do we learn about the gospel from this passage?
7. What does it mean to "reverse the gospel"?
8. What does Paul say about those who preach false gospels?
9. How should you pray for those who are preaching the gospel in local churches today? What might be gained through first praying for your church and your city before expanding your prayers to include the nations?
10. How do Paul's words about pleasing Christ, not men, affect you? Do you struggle with the desire to please others rather than Christ? What might you do to fight this sin effectively?

Paul: From Terrorist to Evangelist

GALATIANS 1:11-24

Main Idea: Paul describes how his gospel came not from man but from God and then shares how Jesus transformed his life.

I. **The Origin of Paul's Message (1:11-12)**
II. **The Transformation of Paul's Life (1:13-24)**
    A. His pre-conversion: In need of grace (1:13-14)
    B. His conversion: God's work of grace (1:15-16a)
    C. His post-conversion: Faithfulness to Jesus (1:16b-24)

This chapter is about how God loves to save bad people. Many have been transformed by the saving power of Jesus. Some of them might think, "My testimony is not that powerful. I never sold drugs. I never committed any 'big' sins." But oh, that is where they go wrong! According to Scripture, all of God's people have been rescued. We have been transferred out of darkness into light and have passed from death to life. All of us are beggars in need of grace. No matter how dull we might judge our own stories, we are desperate people in need of the Savior.

In this passage the amazing, powerful, counter-intuitive grace of God is on display. Paul gives us a picture of God's transforming grace by relating his own story, the story of a terrorist-turned-evangelist. Paul was transformed by his encounter with Jesus. He was not just tweaked by it. Like Paul, we need more than a minor adjustment when we come to Christ; we need transformation. Only the gospel transforms people from the inside out.

Paul is also demonstrating his credibility, which was under attack. He points to two truths to show that he is a true apostle whose words should be heard and accepted like those of the other apostles. He emphasizes the origin of his message and shares the story of his conversion. Some of Paul's critics thought that he either made up his message or simply passed along information second hand, making him inferior to the other apostles. Paul shows us that he did not make up his message. Jesus gave it directly to him. Paul did not just borrow the apostles' message; rather, he acted independently from them for a season before finally meeting them and arriving at the conclusion that they all preached the same gospel message. Two themes dominate this section: the origin of Paul's message and the transformation of Paul's life.

The Origin of Paul's Message
GALATIANS 1:11-12

What is clear in verses 11-12 is that Paul's message was derived from God's revelation, not human imagination. He says his gospel "is not based on human thought." Then he adds, "I did not receive it from a human source." He goes further: "I was not taught it, but it came by a revelation from Jesus Christ," which echoes Galatians 1:1. In verse 17 he adds, "I did not go up to Jerusalem" either, to learn from "those who had become apostles." Instead, Paul could say that he received his message directly from Jesus. Paul met the risen Christ and received his message from Him.

Man did not invent the gospel. It comes from God. It is therefore the standard by which we measure every other set of ideas and every other religion and philosophy.

If you think about it, you have to admit that we would not make this gospel up. If we were given the power to determine how one earned God's favor and a place in heaven, we would make up a scoring system, something that emphasized human works. Why? Because the natural default mode of the human heart is works-righteousness. The message of grace—that the work has already been done—is counter-intuitive. Grace offends our natural sensibilities. Works-righteousness is motivated by unbelief. We do not naturally trust grace. We want control. This supports the reality that people did not make up the gospel of grace; it came from God.

The gospel of grace is like water: people did not invent it, and people cannot live without it. We are spiritually thirsty creatures in need of the living water of the gospel. As believers, we need to keep drinking from this well of grace. Many Christians think they should move on from the gospel—as if there is something more important that Christ's work. No, keep drinking more of grace; keep working the gospel into your heart. You will be prepared to tell unbelievers that what they desperately need is not good advice or moral improvement, but the good news from God about new life in Jesus.

Where do you get your beliefs? It is imperative that you get your beliefs from the right source. Consider the frustration of having a GPS lead you somewhere other than the right destination. My sister and her family were trying to visit us one time when their GPS led them into a brick wall at the end of a one-way street. They were trusting in that GPS as their source for getting to my home, but their chosen system was faulty. Make sure you are trusting in the right source: Jesus. Do not trust in the law of the Pharisees, who "tie up heavy loads" and place them on people (Matt 23:4). Instead, trust in the One who said, "Come to Me . . . and I will give you rest" (Matt 11:28). Listen to Him! Paul presents this message of the gospel, which he got from Jesus Himself. Now we have been entrusted with it that we also may pass it on to others.

The Transformation of Paul's Life
GALATIANS 1:13-24

Paul's conversion is a good reminder for all of us about the difference Jesus Christ can make in a sinner's life (1 Tim 1:15). Even though his story is unique, we will still find important similarities between his experiences and our own. Let us look at his pre-conversion, his conversion, and his post-conversion.

His Pre-Conversion: In Need of Grace (vv. 1:13-14)

We notice first that Paul, like us, was in need of grace. Paul mentions that he **persecuted believers**. He writes, "I persecuted God's church to an extreme degree." In other words, Paul was a terrorist. He approved the martyrdom of the Christian servant, Stephen (Acts 8:1). He dragged Christians to prison (Acts 8:3), and he cast his vote against Christians (Acts 26:10). In fact, Paul was on his way to persecute Christians further when Jesus spoke to him on the Damascus Road. But that encounter with the risen Christ changed him.

Prior to that, Paul's actions against the church were "extreme." Garlington says that Josephus used this language to "denote the burning of villages and towns of Idumaea by Simon Bar Giora" (Schreiner, *Galatians*, 99). Paul adds that he "tried to destroy [the church]." Paul wanted to stamp out Christianity. He was totally convinced that he was doing a good thing and that Christianity was false. In 1 Timothy he referred to himself as a "blasphemer," "persecutor," "arrogant man," ᵥᶜ   ᵤners (1 Tim 1:13-16). He was a violent guy before

.. ᵥ-conversion experience also involved his belonging
ᵥ   **tradition**. He writes, "I advanced in Judaism beyond many
coᵢ   poraries . . . because I was extremely zealous for the traditions of
my ancestors." Paul was a rising superstar in Judaism. He was an honor
student of Gamaliel (Acts 5:34; 22:3).

The word *traditions* refers to Paul's life as a Pharisee. He was a
Pharisee of Pharisees (Phil 3:5; Acts 26:5). This meant that he wasn't
just following Old Testament traditions, but also other traditions that
developed over time. He mentions his religious zeal. Before Paul's
conversion, he thought he was doing the right thing by persecuting
believers. Schreiner (*Galatians*, 100) compares him to Old Testament
characters like Phinehas (Num 25:11), who displayed zeal for observance
to the law when he slew an Israelite man and Midianite woman with a
spear because they were engaging in immoral sexual relations. He was
also compared to Elijah, who displayed zeal by slaying the prophets of
Baal (1 Kgs 19:10,14). Paul probably saw himself as a modern day hero
of the Pharisees.

Paul is a classic example of a person who was sincere in his
misdirected beliefs before becoming a Christian. Sincerity cannot bring
you to salvation if you do not sincerely believe in the truth. You can be
sincerely wrong. You can be consumed with religion and miss Jesus. Paul
was in a desperate situation; we would perhaps look at him and say, "He
is beyond the hope of the gospel." John Stott says,

> Now a man in that mental and emotional state is in no mood
> to change his mind, or even to have it changed for him by
> men. No conditioned reflex or other psychological device
> could convert a man in that state. Only God could reach
> him—and God did! (*Message of Galatians*, 32)

Do you marvel at the fact that God saved you? Do you believe He can
save the worst of sinners? Behold Paul, a terrorist, turning into Christ's
evangelist. What grace!

His Conversion: God's Work of Grace (vv. 15-16a)

Work the truths of verses 15-16a into your heart. Consider the work of
God in the conversion and commission of Paul. We might break it down
into four parts.

Conversion involves God's intervention. We read of that glorious word "but" in verse 15: "But when God, who from my birth set me apart and called me by His grace . . ." After painting a picture of his lost condition in verses 13-14, Paul describes how God interrupted his life by His grace. This text reminds us of other verses where "but" signals a significant message. Ephesians 2:4 and Titus 3:4 further prove that "but . . . God" is a wonderful word of hope!

The gospel is a rescue mission! God intervened in the life of Paul, and He has done the same for all believers. See this gospel in a conjunction: the word "but" is a word of rescue. We use it a lot to describe the good news of certain situations (Gilbert, *What Is the Gospel?*, 59). For instance,

- The other team scored a touchdown, *but* there was a flag on the play!
- I got in a car wreck, *but* no one was hurt.
- He got hit in the face with the ball, *but* nothing is broken.
- You have cancer, *but* it can be treated.
- I was at my wits' end with this kid, *but* God changed him.
- I was on the verge of suicide, *but* God kept me alive.

Conversion is the act in which our stories receive the holy conjunction, "but."

Conversion involves God's eternal planning. Paul writes, "God, who from my birth set me apart." Paul had been set apart from before the womb to serve as an apostle; his thoughts here are similar to ideas expressed in Jeremiah (Jer 1:5), Isaiah (Isa 49:1), and in Luke's reference to John the Baptist (1:12-17). While recognizing the unique role of these prophets and apostles, we too understand that God has chosen us as a people for Himself as part of His eternal, sovereign, and gracious plan (Eph 1:3-14).

Consider the amazing fact that God called Paul before he was born, yet Paul spent years rebelling against God and persecuting the church. No wonder Paul would say of his conversion that Jesus showed "His extraordinary patience" to him (1 Tim 1:16). Through Paul's pre-conversion time, God remained patient with this terrorist. Are you grateful that our God is patient with us too?

Conversion involves God's gracious calling. Paul says, "God . . . called me by His grace." God called Paul powerfully and effectively, just as He called us to Himself.

Our heavenly Father's call is different from the way we call our kids. My call to my five children is a call of desire that does not always bring about reality. I might say, "Come to dinner." And my kids may say, "Okay." However, ten minutes might pass before they start moving because while I can *call* the children, *getting* them to *move* is another matter. Eventually, I might even need to go to their rooms and make them move.

God's call, on the other hand, is action and God's Word is deed. It is reality. When God says, "Let there be light," there is light. Jesus says, "Silence! Be still!" and it gets still. No need to say, "I invite you to be still" or "I hope you are still." Jesus says, "Lazarus, come out!" He does not have to go into the tomb to do CPR or try to offer an incantation. His word brings life.

If you are a Christian, you have sensed at some point God's powerful calling. You have sensed that something or someone is dealing with you. Maybe it was after a sermon, in your room, or in a worship service. Paul was called on the Damascus Road. How did you respond to God's call?

Consider that this powerful calling is an act of grace. Paul says, God "called me by His grace." We meet this all-important subject in every chapter of Galatians. When asked, "How did you become a Christian?" we must simply say, "It was by grace. Pure grace." Paul was not searching for God; he was actually an enemy of God. The Bible is filled with stories of people who received God's grace and blessing, not because of their goodness, but because of His grace.

I heard pastor Mark Dever tell a story about his relative who said that the church was a "pit of vipers."

To this he replied, "Do you think those outside the church are better?"

She said, "No."

He said, "Well, I don't disagree with you. We are. And we've got room for one more, any time you want to slither on in" ("The Church Is the Gospel Made Visible"). We the church are the company of redeemed sinners, people who have been saved by grace.

Conversion involves seeing the glory of Christ. Paul adds, God "was pleased to reveal his Son to me" (ESV). The wonderful reality of Jesus Christ—crucified, risen, and reigning—was made known to Paul. What an amazing truth: God opens the eyes of believers that they may see "God's glory in the face of Jesus Christ" (2 Cor 4:6).

Paul previously knew Christian teaching, but he did not accept it. The idea of a crucified Messiah was repulsive to him and to Jews in general. Then Christ was revealed to him, and everything changed. You may not have a Damascus Road experience. You probably will not, but you will have a 2 Corinthians 4:6 experience. By His Spirit God makes the reality of Christ known to us. We are blind until God opens our eyes. We should thank God that this is no longer true of us: "the god of this age has blinded the minds of the unbelievers" (2 Cor 4:4), and we should pray for those who are still spiritually blind.

When I took my driver's exam to get a North Carolina license, the lady behind the counter asked me if I needed to wear my glasses when driving. I said, "No. They're not that strong. My eyes are not that bad." She proceeded to tell me to read the first line of numbers on their vision-testing screen. I started laughing when I tried to do it because I had no idea what the numbers were. It turned out that I could not see them without my glasses. At her prompting, I put my glasses on and tried again. I could see perfectly!

Apart from the corrective lens provided to us by the Holy Spirit, we can see nothing. We need His help. Upon our conversion we are made into new creations in Christ Jesus (2 Cor 5:16). We see with new eyes, hear with new ears, and feel with new affections. Rejoice that Christ has been made known to you.

His Post Conversion: Faithfulness to Jesus (vv. 1:16b-24)

What can we apply from Paul's post-conversion life?

Like Paul, we can say that Christ now lives in us (v. 16). The phrase translated "to me" (ESV) could be rendered "in me" (HCSB). Either way, we know that Christ dwells in us based on other verses, such as Galatians 2:20: "Christ lives in me."

The mystery of conversion is that after you come to Christ, you are not yourself but you are yourself. There is a new "I." "I no longer live, but Christ lives in me" (2:20). You have a new identity and a new source of power.

Once you become a Christian, you do not then try to live in your own power. You live the same way you enter. Notice Galatians 3:3. Paul says, "After beginning with the Spirit, are you now going to be made complete by the flesh?" We live by the Spirit. Every true Christian has Christ dwelling on the inside. The opposite is also true: "If anyone does not have the Spirit of Christ, he does not belong to Him" (Rom 8:9).

We also share in the responsibility of making Christ known to others (vv. 16-24). Paul said the purpose of his calling was "so that I could preach Him among the Gentiles" (v. 16). Notice the purpose clause, "so that." Paul was not converted just for his own benefit. His conversion came with a commission (cf. Ps 67:1-2). And so does ours! Peter writes, "But you are a chosen race, a royal priesthood, a holy nation, a people for His possession, *so that you may proclaim* the praises of the One who called you out of darkness into His marvelous light" (1 Pet 2:9, emphasis added).

Paul's life was not easy, but it was purposeful. And I would rather have a difficult life with purpose than an easy life that is meaningless. Think of Jeremiah, Isaiah, and John the Baptist, all guys whose calling preceded their time in the womb. They had hard, tear-filled lives. But they were meaningful lives.

Paul reveals his own experience of being converted and then preparing for a life of public proclamation. In so doing, he shows that he acted independently of the apostles. He did not need anyone to confirm this message. He mentions his journey to Arabia in verse 17.

Galatians adds to what is missing in Acts. Paul started by proclaiming Christ in the synagogue in Damascus (Acts 9:19-22) and then went to Arabia. This fact is not mentioned in Acts, though it may be alluded to in 9:23a: "After many days had passed." Paul then returned to Damascus (probably Acts 9:23b-25) and then went to Jerusalem (Acts 9:26).

Paul's reference to "three years" (Gal 1:17-18) likely meant that three years had passed since his conversion, after which he met with the apostles. Some believe this corresponds to the three years the disciples spent with Jesus. But during this time Paul was probably preaching, and he was alone.

Three years of silence is a long time, right? Some of you think you are in a desert. Remember that others in the Bible like Moses, Nehemiah, and even Jesus endured "silent years." Waiting time is not wasted time. God wastes nothing in the lives of His servants.

Paul goes to Jerusalem for a very brief visit (Gal 1:18-20) to meet Peter (also called Cephas) and James. According to Acts 9:28-29, Paul spent most of this time preaching. He then goes to Syria and Cilicia (Gal 1:21). Cilicia (Tarsus) was Paul's home territory. The reference to Syria implies that he might have revisited the churches in Damascus.

In verse 22 Paul says that the churches in Judea did not know him personally. They had only heard that this former persecutor was now a preacher. They had heard that he was now preaching the faith that he tried to destroy (v. 23)! Because of this, Paul says, "They glorified God because of me" (v. 24).

Eleven years pass ("14 years" after his conversion) before Paul goes to Jerusalem for an extended stay (2:1). The previous ventures show that he was away from Jerusalem, except during a short visit, thus proving his independence from the apostles. Paul got his message directly from Jesus (cf. 1:11-12).

This passage causes us to stand amazed at God's transforming grace. Paul summarizes God's work to the Corinthians by saying, "Everything is from God" (2 Cor 5:18). To which we say, "Amen." Consider the story of Paul:

- Pre-Conversion: He was a fanatic headed in the wrong direction.
- Conversion: It was all of God's grace from beginning to end.
- Post-Conversion: It was a story of faithful proclamation of Jesus, who gave him the message.

For us, Paul's is a story that shows us that God loves to save bad people. No one is beyond the reach of His amazing grace! This message only comes from God. The gospel is not good advice from man; it is good news from God. Rejoice in this gospel. In Christ, you find what your heart has always longed to find. No other love is this great. No other hope is this secure. No other forgiveness is this complete. No other joy is this deep. No other freedom is this liberating. No other peace is this sweet. All of it is found in the grace that is in Christ Jesus. Do you know this Savior, the fountain of saving grace? Come and drink!

Reflect and Discuss

1. What were Paul's critics saying about him? Summarize his response.
2. From where did the gospel come? How do most religions typically propose a person can find salvation or fulfillment? How is the true gospel different?
3. Describe Paul's conversion. What amazes you about it?
4. Some people today claim that they have received a direct message from God. How should you respond to them?
5. Why should Paul's conversion and commission encourage us?
6. Does Paul attribute his conversion to his own efforts or to God's grace? Explain.
7. What were people saying about Paul's conversion? What does this suggest about the grace of God?

8. Paul's conversion story is traumatic and dramatic, but how is it similar to the conversion experiences of all Christians?
9. Compare this text to 1 Timothy 1:12-17. What about these two testimony accounts most stands out to you?
10. What is the most important lesson you have learned from chapter 1?

Freed through Faith

GALATIANS 2

Main Idea: Only through faith in Christ are we accepted before God and alive to Him.

I. **Freed by Grace**
II. **Three Pictures (2:1-21)**
    A. Legalism: Right behavior with wrong belief (2:1-10)
    B. Hypocrisy: Right belief with wrong behavior (2:11-14)
    C. Faith: Right belief with right behavior (2:15-21)
III. **Faith Alone**
    A. Through faith in Christ, we are accepted before God.
    B. Through faith in Christ, we are alive to God.
IV. **Freed through Faith**

Freed by Grace

The main truth that we saw over and over again in Galatians 1 is this: God's pleasure in you is not based on your performance for Him. Now in one sense that seems freeing; but in another sense, that seems frustrating. You mean I can't do *anything* to please God? In the answer to that question we have the secret, in a sense, to the Christian life.

Although we can't earn God's favor, Scripture does talk about pleasing God. In 2 Corinthians 5:9 Paul says that his aim is "to be pleasing to Him" (cf. 1 Thess 2:4), and he tells believers to have the same purpose (1 Thess 4:1). But if God's pleasure in me is not based on my performance for Him, then how can I please Him? In Galatians 2 there are three different pictures that help us answer this question—two illustrative episodes in Paul's life (vv. 1-10 and 11-14) and then one foundational explanation (vv. 15-21).

Three Pictures

GALATIANS 2:1-21

Legalism (2:1-10)

In verses 1-10 we see **right behavior with wrong belief**. People debate over when this encounter took place. A majority of scholars think this episode coincided with the Jerusalem Council in Acts 15. Others think Paul is referring to a more private meeting that occurred before the Jerusalem Council, which seems more likely. There are similarities between what Galatians 2 describes and what happens in Acts 15, but there are also significant differences. Also, if Paul were writing this letter after the Jerusalem Council, then certainly he would have mentioned the decision of the church leaders in Jerusalem, a decision that decisively denounced the Judaizers. Regardless of your view on the timing of this encounter, the most important point is the actual substance of what happened.

There was a discussion between Paul and some "false brothers" (2:4) over whether or not Titus, a Gentile believer, needed to be circumcised. Remember that the Judaizers were saying, in effect, that in order to be saved, you needed to follow the Jewish law, most notably, the requirement of circumcision. So if Titus was compelled to be circumcised, that would have been a huge victory for the Judaizers and a huge blow to the gospel of grace, since it would be adding human requirements as necessary for salvation. Thankfully, Titus was not compelled to be circumcised, and the leaders of the church in Jerusalem—Peter, James, and John—affirmed Paul not only as an apostle, but also in the gospel of grace he was preaching (v. 9).[1]

In the previous chapter, we defined legalism as working in our own power according to our own rules, ultimately to earn God's favor. The Judaizers were advocating "good" things, which is why we've labeled their actions as right behavior with wrong belief. Circumcision was important in Jewish life, in addition to a variety of other laws established for the people of Israel. As part of God's Word, none of the Old Testament laws were bad in and of themselves. But laws become legalistic when accompanied by the belief that in doing them, in performing these acts, one can earn merit before God.

Today our problem may not be circumcision or Jewish law, but there's a host of things we might do that fall into this right behavior with

---

[1] In verse 10, we see that apostles agreed not only on the gospel, but also on the need to care for the poor (cf. Gal 6:10; Acts 4:34; 2 Cor 8–9; Jas 2:14-17; 1 John 3:16-18). Luther highlights this important ministry: "After the preaching of the gospel, the office and charge of a true and faithful pastor, is to be mindful of the poor. . . . A faithful pastor must have a care for the poor" (*Galatians*, 26:55). Paul says that he "made every effort" to show such mercy. From our observation of the ministry of Jesus, and from our motivation derived from the gospel of Jesus (that He has shown us grace when we were spiritually impoverished), we too should serve the poor with Christlike compassion.

wrong belief category: having a quiet time, studying the Bible, avoiding certain sins, coming to worship, helping other people. All these are good things, but when we do them thinking that we are earning God's favor, we are becoming legalistic. All of us have this tendency; we are all recovering legalists. We are all born with a sinful nature, thinking we can earn our way to God; this legalistic mind-set carries over even after conversion. Paul's words, then, should serve as a warning to professing Christians. We must avoid this kind of legalism.

Hypocrisy (2:11-14)

This picture in verses 11-14 is the reverse of the previous picture. Instead of right behavior with wrong belief, we see **right belief with wrong behavior**. This is one of the most dramatic and tense episodes in all of the New Testament. Paul the apostle publicly confronts Peter the apostle. Some background and context will help us understand what the big deal was between these two men who were each sent out by the Lord Jesus.

The church at Antioch was made up largely of Gentile Christians. When Peter came to this church, he began eating and spending time with them. That may not seem significant, but this was a huge deal for a Jewish man like Peter. For centuries Jews were known for their strict laws and their separation from Gentiles. Under the old covenant, God had established certain dietary laws and other commandments intended to keep the Jews from intermingling with Gentiles and being corrupted by their idolatry and immorality. This made eating with Gentiles particularly precarious. Gentiles ate certain foods that were forbidden (unclean) to the Jews, and even sitting at the table with them was considered by some to be impure. Table fellowship was more than just inviting someone over for a meal; it was often considered to be a sign of acceptance and approval. That's why the Jewish establishment is astonished when they see Jesus eating with tax collectors and sinners (Mark 2:16). But something happened to Peter in Acts 10 that was paradigm-shifting.

The account in Acts 10 begins with a man named Cornelius, a God-fearing Gentile. He had a vision in which an angel told him to send for the apostle Peter to come to his house. (It may have seemed like an unusual request, but when an angel comes to you in a vision, you do what he says!) Cornelius did as the angel instructed, and while this was happening, Peter had a vision:

> *The next day, as they were traveling and nearing the city, Peter went up to pray on the housetop about noon. Then he became hungry and*

wanted to eat, but while they were preparing something, he went into a visionary state. He saw heaven opened and an object that resembled a large sheet coming down, being lowered by its four corners to the earth. In it were all the four-footed animals and reptiles of the earth, and the birds of the sky. Then a voice said to him, "Get up, Peter; kill and eat!"

"No, Lord!" Peter said. "For I have never eaten anything common and ritually unclean!"

Again, a second time, a voice said to him, "What God has made clean, you must not call common." This happened three times, and then the object was taken up into heaven.

While Peter was deeply perplexed about what the vision he had seen might mean, the men who had been sent by Cornelius, having asked directions to Simon's house, stood at the gate. They called out, asking if Simon, who was also named Peter, was lodging there.

While Peter was thinking about the vision, the Spirit told him, "Three men are here looking for you. Get up, go downstairs, and accompany them with no doubts at all, because I have sent them."

Then Peter went down to the men and said, "Here I am, the one you're looking for. What is the reason you're here?"

They said, "Cornelius, a centurion, an upright and God-fearing man, who has a good reputation with the whole Jewish nation, was divinely directed by a holy angel to call you to his house and to hear a message from you." Peter then invited them in and gave them lodging.

The next day he got up and set out with them, and some of the brothers from Joppa went with him. The following day he entered Caesarea. Now Cornelius was expecting them and had called together his relatives and close friends. When Peter entered, Cornelius met him, fell at his feet, and worshiped him.

But Peter helped him up and said, "Stand up! I myself am also a man." While talking with him, he went on in and found that many had come together there. Peter said to them, "You know it's forbidden for a Jewish man to associate with or visit a foreigner. But God has shown me that I must not call any person common or unclean. That's why I came without any objection when I was sent for. So I ask: Why did you send for me?"

Cornelius replied, "Four days ago at this hour, at three in the afternoon, I was praying in my house. Just then a man in a dazzling robe stood before me and said, 'Cornelius, your prayer has been heard, and your acts of charity have been remembered in God's sight. Therefore send someone to Joppa and invite Simon here, who is also named Peter. He is lodging in Simon the tanner's house by the sea.' Therefore I immediately sent for you, and you did the right thing in coming. So we are all present before God, to hear everything you have been commanded by the Lord."

Then Peter began to speak: "Now I really understand that God doesn't show favoritism, but in every nation the person who fears Him and does righteousness is acceptable to Him. He sent the message to the Israelites, proclaiming the good news of peace through Jesus Christ— He is Lord of all. (Acts 10:9-36)

Peter preached the gospel to Cornelius and his household, and Acts 10:44-48 tells us the result: the Holy Spirit was poured out on Gentiles (which had huge implications). But not everyone was pleased. We read that "those who stressed circumcision" (Acts 11:1-3) were incensed, saying, "You visited uncircumcised men and ate with them!" However, when Peter explained that upon believing in the Lord Jesus Christ the Gentiles had received the gift of the Holy Spirit—the same Holy Spirit that had been poured out upon believing Jews—there was a different reaction: "When they heard this they became silent. Then they glorified God, saying, 'So God has granted repentance resulting in life even to the Gentiles!'" (Acts 11:18). With this background in mind, Paul's confrontation of Peter in Galatians 2:11-14 makes more sense.

Galatians 2:12 says that Peter used to eat with the Gentiles, but because he feared the "circumcision party," he stopped eating with Gentiles and began separating himself from them. And this was the apostle who had brought the gospel to the Gentiles in Acts 10! Other believers began following Peter's lead, including Barnabas, who had helped start the church at Antioch. The implication of Peter's actions was that the Gentiles may not be fully acceptable before God. The key phrase here is: "they were deviating from the truth of the gospel" (2:14). This was right belief with wrong behavior, hypocrisy. Peter knew the gospel and believed the gospel, but his actions didn't reflect the gospel, so Paul called him out.

Today we're not dealing with issues of whether or not Jews and Gentiles should eat together or what kind of food they're eating, but we've got plenty of inconsistencies. There is much in our wealthy, self-indulgent lifestyles that is not in line with the truth of the gospel. This too is hypocrisy. If someone claims to follow the Savior who came to preach good news to the poor and the powerless, yet he or she ignores the poor and the powerless, that's out of line with the gospel. In the same way, if someone is following Christ but living in sexual immorality, there's hypocrisy there, and it should be confronted biblically. Remember, it's not legalistic for believers to confront sin and hypocrisy, even if it's the apostle Peter who must be confronted.

Galatians reminds us how easily we drift toward both legalism and hypocrisy. On the one hand, we think that by doing good things we earn favor before God, legalism. Then on the other hand, we claim to have the gospel of grace but live just like the rest of the world, hypocrisy. We need to avoid both of these errors, which only the Word can help us do.

One of the issues that Paul confronts in Galatians 2 is a two-tiered system of Christianity that was threatening to emerge in the first century: Jews on one side and Gentiles on the other. The Jews claimed that they had more favor before God because they observed the law, thus making the Gentiles feel like second-class Christians. Sometimes the situation was reversed, as in Romans 14, where those who observed the law were looked down upon. Either way, we must guard against a divisive mind-set; there are no second-class Christians in God's kingdom. In our own context, we must reject a kind of two-tiered Christianity with divisions such as

- those who go on mission trips and those who don't;
- those who give a certain amount of money and those who don't;
- or those who drink (in moderation) and those who don't.

Now this doesn't mean we don't encourage one another to follow Christ and to obey the mission of Christ. There ought to be practical ways for that to happen in churches, such as small group participation or going on a mission trip, but we're not in a competition to see who can get the most favor before God. We want to lock arms with other believers in order to avoid legalism and hypocrisy. Within our local churches, we must point one another to the gospel and to the truth of God's Word.

Faith (2:15-21)

We now come to the third picture in this passage that helps us understand what it means to please God. In verses 15-21 Paul describes **right belief with right behavior.** How do you bring these two together? The key word in these verses is *faith.* Everything revolves around faith. Not faith plus anything else; simply faith. Justification is by faith alone.

Faith Alone

In these verses we see two massively important fruits, or results, of faith.

Through Faith in Christ, We Are Accepted before God

In verses 15-16 Paul reminds Peter that they, as Jews, did not find salvation through the law, but through faith in Christ. If righteousness comes through the law, Paul says, then Christ's death was "for nothing" (v. 21). To go back and live as if the law saves after you've been saved through faith in Christ is, in Paul's words, to "rebuild the system I tore down" (v. 18). Paul reminds Peter that God has accepted the Gentiles, even though they aren't circumcised and they don't eat what the old covenant says to eat. And if God has accepted them, so should they (Paul and Peter). Through faith in Christ, Jews *and* Gentiles are accepted before God.

Along with faith, the other key term in these verses is *justified*. **We are justified by faith**. The term *justified* appears four times in verses 16-17. It comes from the same word in the Greek that is translated "righteousness" in verse 21. A number of common New Testament terms come from this same root: justify, justification, just, righteousness, righteous. Justify is a "mega-word" in Christianity. Luther claimed that justification by faith alone is the doctrine upon which the church stands or falls (Sproul, *Acts*, 266). Calvin referred to it as "the hinge upon which everything turns" (ibid.). The doctrine of justification was at the heart of the Reformation, and it's at the heart of Christianity.

Luther said the following of justification:

> And this is the truth of the Gospel. It is also the principal article of all Christian doctrine, wherein the knowledge of all godliness consisteth. Most necessary it is, therefore, that we should know this article well, teach it unto others, and beat it into their heads continually. (Luther, *Commentary*, 206)

That may sound a little forceful, but this is exactly what Paul seems to be doing over and over again in Galatians. He is driving home the point that justification is indispensable in terms of how we think of the gospel and the Christian life.

So what does justification mean? We'll break down the following definition:

> *Justification is the gracious act of God by which God declares a sinner righteous solely through faith in Jesus Christ.*

First, **justification is the gracious act of God**. At the end of verse 16, Paul alludes to the following:

> Lᴏʀᴅ, *hear my prayer.*
> *In Your faithfulness listen to my plea,*
> *and in Your righteousness answer me.*
> *Do not bring Your servant into judgment,*
> *for no one alive is righteous in Your sight.* (Ps 143:1-2)

The psalmist is at the end of himself, and he knows that no one is righteous before God, nor is there anything in man that can make him right before God. Nothing in us warrants, merits, initiates, or causes God to save us. Justification is all about grace, which means that faith itself is evidence of grace. Therefore, we've got to be careful not to make faith into a work of the law, so to speak. Yet I fear that's what we've done with things such as formulaic prayers which, when recited, are supposed to result in conversion. If we're not careful, "Do this work and you'll be saved" is what we're communicating to people. But faith is not a work we muster up. Faith itself is evidence of grace. Justification is a gracious act of God that we need Him to take.

Next, justification is the gracious act of God **by which God declares**. Justification is a declaration. The word picture is that of a judge declaring his judgment. This is important because justification is an act, not a process whereby we're more justified tomorrow than we are today. It's a once-for-all declaration. And once you're declared "justified," or "righteous," you're justified forever. That's why Romans 5:1 says, "Therefore, since we have been declared righteous by faith, we have peace with God through our Lord Jesus Christ."

God the judge makes a declaration in justification, and that declaration involves **a sinner**. This is guilty man standing before holy God. This was a crucial point for Paul, particularly in the context of justification. When Paul first encountered Christ, he realized that God's judgment was due him, not simply for his wickedness, but even for his goodness. If that sounds strange, consider Paul's pre-conversion spiritual resume:

> *circumcised the eighth day; of the nation of Israel, of the tribe of Benjamin, a Hebrew born of Hebrews; regarding the law, a Pharisee; regarding zeal, persecuting the church; regarding the righteousness that is in the law, blameless.* (Phil 3:5-6)

Paul had spent his entire life seeking to obey the law of God, trying to be good. Yes, he was persecuting the church, but that's because he perceived the church to be opposed to the old covenant. He was zealous to keep God's commands. But when he encountered Christ, Paul realized something life-changing: he wasn't good. That is, even his so-called goodness wasn't good enough. That's why he says, "Because of Him I have suffered the loss of all things and consider them filth" (Phil 3:8). All our self-generated "goodness" is actually filthy in the sight of God. That's what makes the next aspect of justification so amazing.

In justification, God takes a sinner, a guilty sinner, and declares him **righteous**. The holy judge of the universe takes a sinner who is in willful rebellion, deserving only of a guilty verdict, and says, "Not guilty." Justification is the opposite of condemnation. It includes God's once-for-all forgiveness of sins and His unchangeable declaration that we are righteous in His sight. You are at peace with God. You're innocent. You're not guilty anymore. This is the gospel! But how? How does this happen? Better yet, how *can* this happen? How can a sinner be declared righteous?

Justification is **solely through faith in Jesus Christ**. God the judge takes the righteousness of Christ and credits it to your account when you put your trust in Christ. Paul puts it this way: "He made the One who did not know sin to be sin for us, so that we might become the righteousness of God in Him" (2 Cor 5:21). We are guilty, deserving of death, but our accounts were credited to Jesus, who bore God's holy wrath on the cross. In turn, by His death on the cross, Christ has made a way for His righteousness to be credited to us. But this righteousness isn't credited to us by our own attempts to add to Christ's finished work. That misses the point. We are justified by trusting in Jesus—by faith. Not faith plus what we do, but faith alone in Christ. Consider Question 60 of the *Heidelberg Catechism*, which describes the Protestant understanding of justification:

Question: How are you righteous before God?

Answer: Only by true faith in Jesus Christ. Although my conscience accuses me that I have grievously sinned against all God's commandments, have never kept any of them, and am still inclined to all evil, yet God, without any merit of my own, out of mere grace, imputes to me the perfect satisfaction, righteousness, and holiness of Christ. He grants these to me as if I had never had nor committed any sin, and as if I myself had accomplished all the obedience which Christ has rendered for me, if only I accept this gift with a believing heart.

The story is told about a wealthy Englishman who purchased a Rolls-Royce and took his new car to France. It had been advertised as the car of all cars—a problem-free automobile. But when the man got his car to France, it broke down. So he called the Rolls-Royce folks in England. They flew a mechanic to France to fix the man's car. Of course, the man expected to get an expensive bill from Rolls-Royce, since they had flown all the way out of the country to fix his car. But months passed by and he never heard from them. So finally he wrote to them and said, "I can pay the bill, just send it to me." Rolls-Royce sent him a note back that said, "I'm sorry, sir, but we have no record of anything ever having gone wrong with your car." To his surprise, the bill was clean.

This is what happens when someone believes the gospel. When you place your faith in Christ and receive His forgiveness and righteousness, God looks at you and says, "I have absolutely no record of anything ever having gone wrong in your life." Praise God for His grace!

Keep in mind, however, that justification is not the same as sweeping sin under the rug and pretending it never existed. God knows it exists. Sin has a penalty, but that penalty has been paid. And the record of your sins was put on the cross of God's Son. That's why we are accepted before God through faith in Christ.

Does this seem too good to be true? That's what some opponents of the Reformation thought, and it's likely what the Judaizers were thinking. If faith alone in Christ is the only basis for acceptance before God, then doesn't that undermine a life lived for God? Galatians 2 has an answer for this objection.

Through Faith in Christ, We Are Alive to God

In verses 18-19 Paul warns against trusting in Christ and then returning to live like your acceptance before God is based on following the law. In verse 19 Paul tells us why he died to the law: "so that I might live for God." Not only are we justified by faith, but **we live by faith**. Paul had no room for a salvation that consists of praying a prayer, supposedly trusting in Jesus, and then living your life the same after that. Impossible. Faith isn't just for *receiving* salvation; it's also for enabling us to *live out* salvation. We live every day, every moment, by faith. This follows from verse 20: "And I no longer live, but Christ lives in me. The life I now live in the body, I live by faith in the Son of God, who loved me and gave Himself for me."

In verse 19 Paul spoke of *dying* to the law, and now in verse 20 he speaks of *living* by faith. So are we dead or alive? To answer that question, we need to consider Christ's death on the cross. There is obviously a sense in which this only involved Christ: He alone could pay the price for all our sin; He alone could bear the full weight of the wrath of God. But in another sense, we share in what happened on the cross. We have been crucified with Christ. The Puritan William Perkins said,

> We are in mind and meditation to consider Christ crucified: and first, we are to believe that he was crucified for us. This being done, we must go yet further, and as it were spread ourselves on the cross of Christ, believing and withal beholding ourselves crucified with him. (Perkins, *Galatians*, 124)

Similarly, Paul says in Romans 6:3 that we've been baptized into Christ's death, meaning that we have died with Him. So what does that mean? It means **we die to sin**—its penalty, power, and dominion. All our sin—past, present, and future—has been paid for on the cross. Christ has taken all of it. So when a Christian sins, God doesn't say, "You're not justified anymore." No, your justification is sealed; you have died to sin. God's declaration is final.

We not only die to sin when we trust in Christ, but **we die to ourselves**. Paul says, "I no longer live" (Gal 2:20). This is where the easy-believism that is being sold today as the gospel is completely undercut. You don't just believe intellectually that Jesus died on the cross for your sins. No, when you place your faith in Christ, you die with Christ. Your heart of stone is crushed, your pride is shattered, and your life is surrendered. You die to your old self that was dominated by sin. In verse 16 Paul speaks of having believed "in Christ Jesus." That word "in" literally carries the idea of faith *into* Christ Jesus. This is more than just assent to the fact that Jesus lived and died; this is running into Christ for mercy.

And when we do, **He covers our sin**. He takes all our sin upon Him and His blood covers it. Paul says Christ died for us while we were still sinners, such that we have been "declared righteous by His blood" (Rom 5:8-9). So Jesus covers our sin, and **He changes our lives**. When Paul says he has been crucified with Christ, he's virtually saying, "It's not the same 'me' anymore. It's not the 'I' that tried to work for God and failed every time, nor the 'I' that thought the world revolved around him. The pride of the old 'I' directed everything to focus on self-esteem, self-confidence, self-direction, and self-exaltation. And it lived for personal pleasure and position. But my life is no longer about me," Paul says, "because Christ lives in me." This is where the key of faith comes in.

Despite how we normally think about Christianity, **we are not in debt to Christ**. We typically reflect on what He did in the past on the cross, which is obviously a good thing to do, but if we're not careful, we will leave it there and start to think, *Jesus has done this for me, so what can I now do for Him?* The reason we must be careful here is because Jesus hasn't stopped *doing* for you. You're not paying Him back, because He's still paying you. **We are indwelt by Christ!** Christ is in us. And the Christian life is not so much about you and I living for Christ as it is trusting Christ to live for us and through us and in us. This is faith. By faith we are accepted before God, and by faith we are alive to God because we are attached to Christ. Consider voices from the past and the present on this crucial truth:

- By faith you are so cemented to Christ that He and you are as one person, which cannot be separated but remains attached to Him forever (Martin Luther cited in Ryken, *Galatians*, 74).
- [Paul, and by implication any Christian,] does not live by his own life, but is animated by the secret power of Christ; so that Christ may be said to live and grow in him (Calvin, *Commentaries*, vol. 21, 74).
- There was a day when I died, *utterly* died . . . died to George Müller, his opinions, preferences, tastes and will—died to the world, its approval or censure—died to the approval or blame even of my brethren and friends—and since then I have studied only to show myself approved unto God (Pierson, *George Müller*, 367).[2]
- Oh, it is joy to feel Jesus living in you . . . to find your heart all taken up by Him; to be reminded of His love by *His* seeking communion with you at all times, not by your painful attempts to abide in Him. He is our life, our strength, our salvation. . . .

---

[2] This was Müller's reply when he was asked about the secret to his effectiveness in ministry. George Müller helped multitudes of orphans through a ministry that did not solicit money, but instead relied solely of prayer.

I am no longer anxious about anything . . . for He, I know, is able to carry out His will, and His will is mine. . . . And His resources are mine, for He is mine, and is with me and dwells in me (Taylor, *Spiritual Secret*, 179, 162–63).

This is the key to the Christian life: faith in Christ—not just the Christ who died on the cross for you, but the Christ who lives in you. We live by faith when we believe Christ every moment of every day. We believe Him to be our sustenance and our strength. We believe Him to be our love and joy and peace. We believe Him to be our satisfaction—more than money and houses and cars and stuff. We believe Christ to be our purity and our holiness and our power over sin. This is Christianity: believing Christ to be everything you need for every moment you live. You live by faith in the Son of God.

Freed through Faith

So how do you please God? How can you obey all these radical commands of Christ that we see in the Gospels and throughout the New Testament? The answer is you can't. You need Christ to do it. And He's there. So trust Him. And realize that God's pleasure in you is not based on your performance for Him; instead, **God's pleasure in you is based on Christ's performance for you**. And remember, even after we have been accepted by God, our good works are still the result of Christ's work in us. We must trust Him daily to produce in us that which pleases God.

But how do you know He'll give you everything you need to follow His Word? You know this because, in the words of Paul, He loves you and He gave Himself for you (v. 20). Paul gets extremely personal here, and it's as if he invites you to say, "Christ loves me." You can trust Jesus to be everything you need or want and to be your life because **He is passionate about you**. He loves you. It's good to remember that God's passion is for the world and for all peoples, and that Christ died for all peoples in all nations. That's biblical Christianity. But I want to remind you that Christ died on the cross for *you*.

Jesus is not only passionate about you, but **He has paid a price for you**. He gave Himself for you on the cross so that His life, with all of its present and eternal benefits, might be yours. So let's trust Him. We are saved by grace alone through faith alone in Christ alone.

Reflect and Discuss

1. If someone is a good employee, an unselfish friend, and an advocate for the poor, should we consider that person a Christian? Explain.
2. How would you counsel someone who claimed to believe in justification by faith but showed no signs of love for Christ?
3. Briefly explain the doctrine of justification by faith in terms that an unbeliever with no Bible knowledge could understand.
4. Why does it rob God of glory when we add to faith other requirements for justification? How do people attempt to justify themselves today?
5. Why is it so significant that we view justification as a once-for-all declaration and not a process?
6. How is the justification of a sinner different from having one's sins ignored or swept under the rug?
7. Faith is clearly crucial for our justification, but what role does it play in our lives after that point?
8. What's the potential danger in the following statement: Jesus has done so much for me, so now I must work for Him?
9. How should the reality of Christ's indwelling presence affect your everyday life?
10. Luther referred to justification by faith as the doctrine on which the church stands or falls. Why does this doctrine affect everything about the church's life and witness?

Free in Christ

GALATIANS 3:1-25

Main Idea: God's covenant with Moses does not contradict His covenant with Abraham, but rather complements it, and both covenants find their fulfillment in Christ and His salvation.

I. **God's Covenant with Abraham**
   A.   By grace alone, God blesses His people.
   B.   Through faith alone, God's people receive His blessing.
II. **God's Covenant with Moses**
   A.   We all disobey the law of God.
   B.   We all deserve the wrath of God.
III. **God's Covenant through Christ**
   A.   Jesus fulfills the law of Moses.
   B.   Jesus completes the promise to Abraham.

Some time ago I trained for a marathon, which meant several months of training runs. The training run on one particular day was supposed to be 12 miles, but just before I started I decided to go ahead and run 13 miles in order to complete a half-marathon. Just to be clear, 13 miles is a long way for me to run . . . and it would end up being even longer than I thought. Unfortunately, right around the 12-mile mark, I took a wrong turn. All of a sudden, my 12-mile-turned-13-mile run turned into something closer to a 17-mile run. I would say that my legs felt like Jell-O, but Jell-O doesn't hurt like that. Unsuspectingly, I had gotten in over my head.

That's precisely how Galatians 3 can make us feel as we try to understand this highly-debated passage. Here we have one of the more complicated chapters in all of Paul's writings. One commentator noted that there may be up to 300 different interpretations for verse 20 alone (Lightfoot, *Galatians*, 146)! Needless to say, reading this text can feel like an interpretive marathon, and while it's not easy, it is worth the effort. But it's not for the faint of heart. If all we want is a quick and simple, entertaining, give-me-a-practical-tip-on-how-to-live-a-good-life message from the Bible, we'll skip over texts like Galatians 3. But if we want to know God, we'll dive in, or even better, we'll *delight in* texts like these. I would describe this chapter as three mountain peaks that appear back to back to back. You climb the first two peaks, which takes a lot of effort; then you climb the third and final peak, and it seems like Mount Everest. It's tall and it requires hard work to scale, but when you get to the top, you look around and think, *Yes*—this *is what I came for.*

In Galatians 3 Paul takes us on a history lesson through the Old Testament. The first peak he talks about deals with Abraham, and the second peak deals with Moses. The third and final peak leads us to Christ. Rather than going verse-by-verse through this passage, we'll consider this text through the lens of these three peaks. Paul comes back to these peaks, these themes, over and over again, from different angles and in different ways.

So, are you ready to climb?

God's Covenant with Abraham

The first of the three mountain peaks we come to in this text concerns the covenant God made with Abraham. In this Old Testament story, **God's promise shows us the necessity of faith**, a theme that runs throughout Galatians. Recall that Paul was addressing a church where false teachers known as Judaizers were saying that in order to be a Christian, you needed to follow the Old Testament law in addition to believing in Christ. Circumcision, and possibly other Jewish rules and customs, was being advocated by these Judaizers. Paul introduced the doctrine of justification by faith alone in the previous chapter (2:15-21), a doctrine that's at the heart of this letter, and now he defends this doctrine in chapter 3. He starts by asking the Galatians six rapid-fire questions in the first five verses. These questions are really summed up by the question in verse 2: "Did you receive the Spirit by the works of the law or by hearing with faith?" The Galatian believers needed to recognize that they received the Spirit by faith, not by the works of the law.

To demonstrate his point in verses 1-5, Paul introduces Abraham (his name was originally Abram until God changed it in Gen 17:5), the father of God's people, in verse 6. Abraham is significant for a number of reasons, not least because he was the first man that God commanded to be circumcised (Gen 17:9-14). The first Old Testament text Paul quotes in relation to Abraham is Genesis 15:6, which we'll see more about below. Then he quotes from Genesis 12:3, where God first called

Abraham. We've got to go back to this passage to remember how God's people of faith began to take shape.

> *The LORD said to Abram:*
>> *Go out from your land, your relatives, and your father's house to the land that I will show you. I will make you into a great nation, I will bless you, I will make your name great, and you will be a blessing.* (Gen 12:1-3)

By Grace Alone, God Blesses His People

God promised to bless Abraham, though keep in mind that Abraham had done nothing to deserve this privilege. The future patriarch was a pagan man in all likelihood, yet God graciously came to him. Abraham's story reminds us that by grace alone, God blesses His people. As the story continues, notice that Abraham didn't make a covenant with God; rather, God made a covenant with Abraham. This is even clearer in the other passage Paul quotes from, Genesis 15:6. God was promising to bless all nations through Abraham, but at this point Abraham didn't have a single heir! Sarah, his wife, was unable to have a child, which was obviously a huge problem. Here is the account of God's promise and Abraham's faith:

> *After these events, the word of the LORD came to Abram in a vision:*
>> *Do not be afraid, Abram. I am your shield; your reward will be very great.*
>
>> *But Abram said, "Lord GOD, what can You give me, since I am childless and the heir of my house is Eliezer of Damascus?" Abram continued, "Look, You have given me no offspring, so a slave born in my house will be my heir."*
>
>> *Now the word of the LORD came to him: "This one will not be your heir; instead, one who comes from your own body will be your heir." He took him outside and said, "Look at the sky and count the stars, if you are able to count them." Then He said to him, "Your offspring will be that numerous."*
>
>> *Abram believed the LORD, and He credited it to him as righteousness.* (Gen 15:1-6)

As God extends His grace to Abraham, **this grace is expressed in radical promises**. Abraham's offspring will be as numerous as the stars in the sky. That's a stout promise, especially when you realize that

Abraham was 99 years old and Sarah would be 90 years old by the time the child arrived (Gen 17:17). You don't have to do the math on this one: the prospects for offspring were not looking good. But this promise wasn't really about Abraham and Sarah; it was about God, *His* grace and *His* promises.

In Genesis 15 we read about the covenant God made with Abraham. In that day, you would confirm an oath or covenant with someone by cutting animal sacrifices in half and placing them in two rows (the rows faced one another with space in between). Both parties would then walk together through the sacrifices, but something unique happened when this covenant was made (Gen 15:7-21). When God enacted the covenant, Abraham was asleep. Only the Lord passed between the pieces, such that *He* made the covenant, and He did it based on His grace, not Abraham's works. Abraham's righteousness, according to Genesis 15:6, was "credited to him." By grace alone, God blesses His people. But how did Abraham receive this blessing?

Through Faith Alone, God's People Receive His Blessing

Grace is not earned. Abraham simply believed God, and it was credited to him as righteousness. He didn't *do* anything; he *believed* something. More appropriately, he believed Someone—God. And he did this in the face of an outlandish promise, namely, that his wife would have a son and through that son's line all the nations of the earth would be blessed.

Paul addresses the relationship of Abraham's righteousness to his circumcision in Romans 4:9-12, a passage that serves as a commentary on Galatians 3. The apostle asks, "In what way then was it credited—while he was circumcised, or uncircumcised? Not while he was circumcised, but uncircumcised" (Rom 4:10). Righteousness was not credited to Abraham after he was circumcised, but before. Abraham's faith was the crucial point.

This has always been the case. Hebrews 11:4 tells us that Abel's sacrifice was more acceptable than Cain's due to his faith. Likewise Enoch, Noah, Abraham, Sarah, Isaac, Jacob, Joseph, Moses, Rahab, the godly judges, kings, prophets, and others throughout the Old Testament received God's blessing through faith, not through what they did (cf. Hebrews 11). In Hebrews, the author states, "Now without faith it is impossible to please God, for the one who draws near to Him must believe that He exists and rewards those who seek Him" (Heb 11:6). It's through faith alone that we receive God's promises.

Imagine that a wealthy man offered you and your family a house in Barbados—no payment, no strings attached, and you can use it whenever you want. It's not only that you don't have to do anything to receive this promise; you *can't* do anything to help this wealthy man fulfill it. The only thing you can do is trust the promise, namely, that when you go to Barbados, there will be a house, and it will have your name on it. Through believing, you will receive. This is the truth that turned Martin Luther's world upside down.

Habakkuk 2:4, a verse Paul quotes in Galatians 3:11, says the following: "But the righteous one will live by his faith." Luther first read Habakkuk 2:4 when he was a monk living in a monastery, but he didn't understand it at the time. Later he went through a period of illness and depression as he imagined himself under the wrath of God. Lying in a bed in Italy, fearing he was about to die, Luther found himself repeating over and over again, "The righteous will live by faith." He recovered and went to Rome, where he visited one of the famous churches there. The pope in that day had promised an indulgence forgiving the sins of any pilgrim who mounted the tall staircase in front of the church. Pay your money, climb the staircase, and you can have your sins or someone else's forgiven. People flocked to climb the staircase on their knees, pausing to pray and kiss the stairs along the way. Luther's son later wrote the following of that experience for his father: "As he (Luther) repeated his prayers on the Lateran staircase, the words of the Prophet Habakkuk came suddenly to his mind: 'The just shall live by faith.' Thereupon he ceased his prayers, returned to Wittenberg, and took this as the chief foundation of all his doctrine" (Boice, *Minor Prophets*, 91). Luther later said, "Before those words broke upon my mind I hated God and was angry with him. . . . But when, by the Spirit of God, I understood those words—'The just shall live by faith!' 'The just shall live by faith!'—then I felt born again like a new man; I entered through the open doors into the very Paradise of God" (ibid., 92).

Faith—faith alone! Abraham believed God, and it was credited to him as righteousness. Believe God, and it will be credited to *you* as righteousness. "That's all?" you ask. That's all! "But doesn't that lead to loose living?" Scripture speaks to this danger as well.

We become righteous before God through faith in Christ, and **this faith is expressed in radical obedience.** What happened after Abraham's faith was credited as righteousness in Genesis 15:6?

He was circumcised; he obeyed because of his faith. Yes, he was justified by faith, but he also began to live obediently by faith. In Genesis 12, right after God promised Abraham great blessing, the patriarch left his father's land and everything that was familiar and went wherever God told him. He lived in tents as a "foreigner in the land of promise" (Heb 11:9). And then in Genesis 22, God told him to sacrifice Isaac, the son God promised and miraculously gave to him. And what did Abraham do? He took his son and raised the knife to sacrifice him—he was going to do it! Listen to God's response:

> Because you have done this thing and have not withheld your only son, I will indeed bless you and make your offspring as numerous as the stars of the sky and the sand on the seashore. (Gen 22:16-17)

God promised to bless Abraham because of his obedience. So does that ruin Paul's argument? No!

God gave Abraham the promise by grace, and Abraham trusted the promise through faith, and that faith led to radical obedience. When you trust God, you do things that seem crazy to the world, not because you're earning salvation, but because you believe God. This is the whole point of Hebrews 11, which we've referenced earlier. Consider the fruit of faith in the lives of a number of Old Testament saints,

> who by faith conquered kingdoms, administered justice, obtained promises, shut the mouths of lions, quenched the raging of fire, escaped the edge of the sword, gained strength after being weak, became mighty in battle, and put foreign armies to flight. Women received their dead—they were raised to life again. Some men were tortured, not accepting release, so that they might gain a better resurrection, and others experienced mockings and scourgings, as well as bonds and imprisonment. They were stoned, they were sawed in two, they died by the sword, they wandered about in sheepskins, in goatskins, destitute, afflicted, and mistreated. The world was not worthy of them. They wandered in deserts and on mountains, hiding in caves and holes in the ground.
>
> All these were approved through their faith, but they did not receive what was promised, since God had provided something better for us, so that they would not be made perfect without us. (Heb 11:33-40)

These men and women were commended for their faith. We often don't live radical lives because we don't have faith. People who are saved by grace alone through faith alone don't sit back and indulge in sin and the ways of this world just like everyone else. Why? Because they believe God. They're not only saved by grace through faith, but they also live by grace through faith. And they risk everything because they know that God is good, that He is sufficient, and that He satisfies. The saints of Hebrews 11 knew that they were "foreigners and temporary residents on the earth," and thus they were "seeking a homeland"; therefore, "God is not ashamed to be called their God" (Heb 11:13,14,16).

John Bunyan, author of the classic allegory *Pilgrim's Progress*, was a member of his church while in his twenties, but by all accounts not a Christian. He struggled to find peace and assurance as he wrestled with his salvation, but he couldn't seem to find it. Then one day it hit him: Christ was his righteousness. And he, John Bunyan, could only be righteous before God by faith. Bunyan writes,

> One day as I was passing into the field . . . this sentence
> fell upon my soul, "Thy righteousness is in heaven." And I
> thought, withal, I saw with the eyes of my soul, Jesus Christ at
> God's right hand. There, I say, was my righteousness; so that
> wherever I was, or whatever I was doing, God could not say of
> me, "He lacks my righteousness"; for that was just before Him.
> I also saw moreover, that it was not my good frame of heart
> that made my righteousness better, nor yet my bad frame that
> made my righteousness worse; for my righteousness was Jesus
> Christ Himself. . . . Now did my chains fall off my legs indeed;
> I was loosed from my afflictions and irons; my temptations also
> fled away; . . . now went I also home rejoicing, for the grace
> and love of God. (Bunyan, *Grace Abounding*, 75–76)

Bunyan came to know that righteousness only comes by faith in Christ, and that freed him. He evidently knew the truth of Galatians 3. Bunyan even said that outside the Bible, Luther's commentary on Galatians was his favorite book of all time (Ryken, *Galatians*, 5). He knew salvation by grace alone through faith alone, so he preached it. And because he preached it, he was thrown into jail. The authorities offered to release him if he would stop preaching, and though Bunyan had a wife and four children, one of whom was blind, he refused to stop preaching. As a result, he spent 12 years in prison. And why would he do that? Because of salvation by grace through faith. He titled his autobiography *Grace Abounding to the Chief of Sinners*, which he wrote in prison.

> I am indeed in prison now
>   In body, but my mind
> Is free to study Christ, and how
>   Unto me, he is kind.
>
> For tho' men keep my outward man
>   Within their locks and bars
> Yet by the faith of Christ I can
>   Mount higher than the stars.
>
> Their fetters cannot spirits tame,
>   Nor tie up God from me;
> My faith and hope they cannot lame,
>   Above them I shall be. (Bunyan, *Complete Works*, 691)

Bunyan illustrates the kind of faith God gives us. It's the kind of faith that comes through His grace, and it leads to radical obedience. The rest of Galatians is going to show us this truth, particularly chapters 5 and 6. We need God to show us how to put grace, faith, and obedience together so that we don't waste our lives on the things of this world, all the while thinking and claiming to believe in grace.

Key Truth

So far we've looked at the first mountain peak in this passage: God's covenant with Abraham. Now Paul moves on in Old Testament history to Moses. It's important to remember that **God's covenant with Moses does not contradict His covenant with Abraham; instead, God's covenant with Moses complements His covenant with Abraham**. Paul says in Galatians 3:15-16 that the law God gave through Moses didn't nullify or replace what He had promised to and through Abraham. It complemented it by serving that promise. The Judaizers recognized the importance of the Abrahamic covenant, but they gave priority to the Mosaic covenant. Instead of looking at the Mosaic covenant through the lens of the Abrahamic covenant, they reversed that order and viewed the Abrahamic covenant through the lens of the Mosaic covenant. This led them to emphasize Moses' obedience to the law as primary. So now, they reasoned, in order to be right with God, we've got to *do* certain things.

In contrast to the Judaizers, Paul tells us that while God's covenant with Moses was important, it didn't nullify what had been promised through Abraham. In fact, what God did with Moses helps us understand what God did with Abraham. The necessity of faith is still there in both covenants. God saves His people by grace through faith, even under the law in the Old Testament. That aspect of God's salvation never changed. So why did God give the law? That's what Paul addresses in Galatians 3:10-25.

God's Covenant with Moses

Key to understanding God's covenant with Moses is a proper understanding of the purpose of the law in the first place. One aspect of this is that **God's law shows us the futility of the flesh**. To clarify, most of Paul's references to the law, including here in Galatians 3, deal with the commandments and requirements God gave to His people through Moses. There were moral laws, such as the Ten Commandments; there were ceremonial laws specifying how you were to worship, what sacrifices to make, what foods to eat or not eat, and what festivals to celebrate; further, there were civil laws outlining procedures and punishments for crimes like murder and adultery. These moral, ceremonial, and civil laws came together to form *the law*. This is important for understanding Galatians 3, because when the law is mentioned, Paul is specifically talking about the Old Testament law revealed to Moses. He's not talking about all of Scripture, which now includes the New Testament, though there's a sense in which the truths he establishes can apply to our understanding of the Bible as the law of God and of the purpose of God's Word in our lives. But in this passage we first need to think about the law in terms of the Old Testament law given through Moses.

Paul starts talking about the law in verse 10, and he begins by talking about what the law can't do. It can't bring life. It can't bring salvation. It can't bring righteousness before God. So then in verse 19 he gets to the obvious question: "Why then was the law given?" In other words, if it can't do those things, then what's the point? Paul answers that question by telling us that the law was given to show us the futility, weakness, and inability of the flesh. When Paul refers to the *flesh* here and elsewhere in Galatians, he usually refers to the sinful nature in us. This is our nature apart from Christ. The flesh says, "I'm the authority in my life. I call the shots, I know what's best, I do what I want to do, and don't tell me any different." This is the mind-set that Adam and Eve took in the garden of Eden in the very beginning: "I can eat this fruit if I want to." What Paul is saying is that the law was given to clarify that the flesh is sinful to the core and in need of salvation.

We All Disobey the Law of God

In our flesh, we all disobey the law of God. This is what Paul is saying here:

> For all who rely on the works of the law are under a curse, because it is written: Everyone who does not continue doing everything written in the book of the law is cursed. (3:10)

He is quoting from Deuteronomy 27:26 to show that the law demands obedience, perfect obedience. Similarly, when Jesus preaches the Sermon on the Mount, recounting various aspects of the Old Testament law, he says, "Be perfect, therefore, as your heavenly Father is perfect" (Matt 5:48). The law shows us that we can't be perfect, because **the law exposes our sin**. To be clear, the law doesn't make us sinners but rather reveals the fact that we are already sinners. It uncovers the sinful heart that is in each of us. In Calvin's words, "The law was given in order to make known transgressions obvious" (Calvin, *Epistles of Paul*, 61).

Giving instructions to children is a good analogy to the law's purpose. My son has a sinful heart, but that heart isn't obvious until I give him a command. Until I say, "Son, do this," and he looks at me and says, "No," his sin isn't put on display. The command brings his disobedient heart to the surface. Similarly, the law of God exposes the sinful heart in each of us.

Not only does the law expose our sin, but also **the law intensifies our sin**. In Galatians 3:19 the apostle says that the law was added "because of transgressions." Although commentators take different views on this verse, a better translation here probably carries the idea that the law was added to *produce* transgressions (Schreiner, *Galatians*, 239–40). It's the same thing Paul says in Romans 5:20, "The law came along to multiply the trespass." The law isn't sinful; it's good. Paul says that it is "holy and just and good" (Rom 7:12). Under the law, the reign of sin expands, thus making its presence felt even more keenly. In this way, the law doesn't make us better; it makes us worse. Our hearts, which resist the law, grow harder and harder apart from the grace of God. This is Paul's point: the law confronts man with his disobedience, his continual disobedience, and exposes his sin, even intensifying it.

We All Deserve the Wrath of God

The result of our sin and our disobedience is that we all deserve the wrath of God. It's not good to be confronted by sin in the presence of a holy God, a God who has no sin and is wholly dead set against sin. The law causes us to tremble before the wrath of God. Luther summed this up when he said,

> The principal point . . . of the law . . . is to make men not better but worse; that is to say, it sheweth unto them their sin, that by the knowledge thereof they may be humbled, terrified, bruised and broken, and by this means may be driven to seek grace. (Luther, quoted in Stott, *Message of Galatians*, 91)

We need grace, Paul says, because **we stand cursed beneath the law**. Verse 10 makes this exact point concerning those who rely on the works of the law. The magnitude of this statement should come across to us as if an announcement had just been made that 100 nuclear warheads were headed right for this country (Piper, *Christ Redeemed Us*). Each of us stands under the curse of the law, the law given by the sovereign judge of the universe.

Again, it's important that we understand God's covenant with Moses. The prior covenant made with Abraham was focused on blessing: "I will bless you. . . . I will bless those who bless you . . . and all the peoples of the earth will be blessed through you" (Gen 12:2-3). But the setting is different when we get to the covenant God gave through Moses. In Deuteronomy 27, which is what Paul references in Galatians 3:10, Moses tells the people of God to divide up between two mountains. They are to face each other and shout pronouncements to each other. One group is supposed to pronounce blessings upon the people of God, while the other group is supposed to pronounce curses. The curses fell on those who dishonored their father and mother, those who led the blind astray, and on those who committed a number of other sins (Deut 27:15-26). And after each of the curses was pronounced, all the people would shout, "Amen!" There were certainly blessings associated with the covenant, but the curses were very prominent. The last curse in Deuteronomy 27:26 is what Paul quotes in Galatians 3:10, the curse that lies on those who do not obey the law.

The law was given to remind us that we are cursed under the judgment of God because we fail to do everything written in the book of the law. We cannot make our own way to God. Notice that Galatians 3 is pronouncing a curse on all people, including those who are trying to obey the law of God, for none can obey it perfectly. The law shows every single one of us that we are cursed beneath it, and as a result, **we stand condemned before God**. The Westminster Shorter Catechism asks: "What does every sin deserve?" Answer: "Every sin deserves God's wrath and curse, both in this life, and that which is to come."[3] That answer may not be popular, but it's true that each of us stands guilty before God's law. And the more you try to obey it—the more you go to church, the more you try to pray, the more you try to be good, the more you try to lead your family the right way—the more the law says, "Guilty."

Does that make you feel helpless—like you can't ever get it right? That's the point. That's why God gave the law: to show us we can't get it right. And that's why we need the law. It's also why we don't shrink back from talking about words like *curse, condemnation, wrath, disobedience,* and *futility*. If no one brings up these words, we *think* we're okay. But we're not. We're desperately in need of a Savior to deliver us from the curse and condemnation and wrath that is due our disobedience and the futility and rebellion of our flesh. Paul says in verse 22 that we're prisoners of sin because of the law, locked up with no way out, chained with no hope of breaking free in our own strength. Verses 23-24 say it this way:

> *Before this faith came, we were confined under the law, imprisoned until the coming faith was revealed. The law, then, was our guardian until Christ, so that we could be justified by faith.*

---

[3] This is Question 84 along with the answer from the Westminster Shorter Catechism (with slightly updated language), which can be found online in a number of places, including at the Center for Reformed Theology and Apologetics (see "Works Cited" for location).

God's Covenant through Christ

So far we've seen the first mountain peak in this text in God's covenant with Abraham, where God's promise shows us the necessity of faith. The second mountain peak came in the covenant with Moses, where the law shows us the futility of the flesh. The third mountain peak is more impressive than Mount Everest; it's God's covenant through Christ.

Jesus Fulfills the Law of Moses

By His death on the cross, **God's Son shows us the price of freedom**. Everything in the Old Testament was building to this reality. When you get to the New Testament—the new covenant—you realize that Jesus fulfills the law of Moses. In verse 19 Paul said that the law was added "because of transgressions *until the Seed to whom the promise was made would come*" (emphasis added). Who's the Seed? Verse 16 tells us: "Now the promises were spoken to Abraham and to his seed. He does not say 'and to seeds,' as though referring to many, but referring to one, 'and to your seed,' *who is Christ*" (emphasis added). Notice the temporary nature of the law; it was given until something else would come (actually, until Someone else would come). The Mosaic Law, with all its ceremonies and rituals and its priesthood and sacrifices, was given until Christ came. It was all a shadow pointing to a substance (Col 2:17). Everything in the law was shouting, "Look to Christ!" As Paul says in Romans 10:4, "For Christ is the end of the law for righteousness."

Jesus came to fulfill the law (Matt 5:17), and in doing so, **He obeyed the law of God for us**. Jesus shows us that the law is good, for He fulfilled it completely (cf. Rom 7:16; 1 Tim 1:8). Jesus alone has a righteousness that is sufficient before God. No other religious teacher, whether in the Bible or in any other religion, can claim a righteousness of his own merit before God. Only Jesus.

Obeying the law on our behalf was an utterly crucial aspect of Christ's work for our salvation, but there's more. **He endured the wrath of God instead of us**:

> *Christ has redeemed us from the curse of the law by becoming a curse for us, because it is written: Everyone who is hung on a tree is cursed. The purpose was that the blessing of Abraham would come to the Gentiles by Christ Jesus, so that we could receive the promised Spirit through faith.* (Gal 3:13-14)

Christ redeemed us. The word *redeemed* was sometimes used in Paul's day to describe the purchase of a slave in order to set him free. Slavery is a great picture of man outside of Christ. There we sit, chained by sin, cursed beneath the law, condemned before God forever. There's nothing we can do. But then we look to Jesus. Perfectly righteous. No condemnation. A lamb without blemish or defect (1 Pet 1:19). And He says, "I'll take the curse for you." That's the beauty of those words "for us" in verse 13, two of the most beautiful words in all of Scripture. Quite literally, Christ became a curse *instead of* us. He was hung on a tree, cursed by God, for us. He shed His blood and endured God's wrath and condemnation for us.

How do you even begin to respond to that? Augustus Toplady's hymn "Rock of Ages" is a good place to start:

> Nothing in my hand I bring,
> Simply to thy cross I cling:
> Naked, come to thee for dress;
> Helpless, look to thee for grace;
> Foul, I to the fountain fly:
> Wash me, Savior, or I die!

The law drives us to our faces to say with Paul, "What a wretched man I am! Who will rescue me from this dying body? I thank God through Jesus Christ our Lord!" (Rom 7:24-25). This is the summit to which the Mosaic covenant points—the crucifixion of Christ where He takes the curse of the law upon Himself.

Jesus Completes the Promise to Abraham

Christ's work on the cross also takes us back further to God's dealings with Abraham. As one from Abraham's line, Jesus completes the promise to Abraham. Jesus is the Seed to which the promise pointed (Gal 3:16,19). Christ perfectly lived the life of faith that is described in Scripture, and He died so that the blessing of God would be made known in all nations (Gen 12:3). Through trusting in Christ, we become children of Abraham, the people of God. Abraham was pointing us to Christ. This is why Jesus said, "Your father Abraham was overjoyed that he would see My day; he saw it and rejoiced" (John 8:56). That's an astounding statement. Abraham was justified by faith in the promise of God, and that promise, ever since the beginning, was pointing to Christ.

The only way to come to God is through Christ and Christ alone. Abraham and every other saved person in the Old Testament had faith that was pointing to Christ. Due to the progressive nature of God's revelation, these Old Testament saints may not have realized all the details about what God was going to do in Christ, but their faith was in the gospel.

By grace alone, He gives salvation to us. Paul continually points out to the Galatians that they have done nothing to merit God's salvation. They did nothing to become children of Abraham. It is the grace of God that saves us, just like it was the grace of God that saved Paul on the road to Damascus. God's grace in the gospel is stunning. It's not a moral improvement program. It's not about rule-keeping or checking off boxes. It's not about being nice to others and getting our relationships and problems fixed so that we can have a successful life. No, it is salvation by grace, full and free.

And how do we receive it today? The same way Abraham did: **Through faith alone, we receive God's Spirit in us.** Paul mentions the gift of the Spirit in verse 14, and it's a reminder that the blessings we receive in the new covenant in Christ are even greater than the blessings of the old covenant. Having the Holy Spirit changes everything. As believers we actually have the living presence of Christ in us. Paul opened this chapter by talking about the Spirit: "Did you receive the Spirit by the works of the law or by hearing with faith?" (v. 2). Later Paul tells us that those who are led by the Spirit are not under the law (5:18). This theme of freedom from the law in Christ is still prominent near the close of chapter 3 in verse 25. And the remainder of Galatians will emphasize just how important the gift of the Spirit is (cf. Rom 8:9).

Reflect and Discuss

1. Why is it important for Christians to study the Old Testament? What are some of the dangers of ignoring the Old Testament?
2. How did God's promise to Abraham highlight the need for faith?
3. What is the relationship between faith and obedience?
4. Read James 2:14-26. How do you reconcile Paul's words about justification by faith with James' words about faith and works?
5. How does the law help us see our sin? How does the law prepare us for grace?

6. What are some ways we look to the law to produce the obedience that only the gospel can bring about?
7. How does the Mosaic covenant complement the Abrahamic covenant?
8. In your own words, explain what it means that Jesus fulfilled the law of Moses.
9. How does God's promise in the Abrahamic covenant to bless all nations relate to Jesus?
10. How might Jesus' relationship to these covenants affect the way you read the Old Testament?

Free as Sons

GALATIANS 3:26–4:7

Main Idea: God has graciously adopted us, giving us the position of sons and the privileges of sonship.

I. **Salvation in Galatians**
   A. We are saved by grace alone through faith alone in Christ alone.
   B. Justification: We are right before God the judge.
   C. Adoption: We are loved by God the Father.
II. **The Adoptive Father**
   A. God sent His Son so that we might receive the position of sons.
      1. Adoption requires someone who comes at the right time.
      2. Adoption requires someone who possesses the right qualifications.
      3. Adoption requires someone who has the right resolve.
   B. God sent His Spirit so that we might experience the privileges of sonship.
      1. We live with a new identity before God.
      2. We enjoy intimacy with God.
      3. We are guaranteed an inheritance from God.

The adoption process is challenging on so many different levels. One of the most challenging things that my wife and I have found has been hearing how people talk about adoption. People can tell that my daughter and one of my sons have been adopted, and when we share their stories, people say, "Oh, that's so nice; now do you also have children of your own?" That's phrase number one *not* to say to an adoptive parent. I want to say, "Come in real close. I have a secret: they're ours!"

Other questions reveal a similar view of adoption. Some people wonder if we care about our children's heritage, and the very question implies that their heritage is thousands of miles away. But the reality is this: their heritage is *here*. Now that doesn't mean that Kazakhstan or China (the countries we have adopted from) are discounted altogether, or that a child who has lived in another country shouldn't have any appreciation for that country. But my son and daughter are Platts, not partly Platts, but fully Platts, with all the heritage that a Platt has. They're in our family in the same way as our other two sons.

Another comment we hear is, "I just don't know if I can love an adopted child like a biological child." There we go, using that distinction again. I guarantee you that the affection that my wife and I have for the children we have adopted is absolutely no different from our affection for the sons we had naturally. They're all our children.

These phrases, myths, and misconceptions about adoption are not just annoyances to parents who have been through the adoption process. They're symptoms of something deeper. They show how little we understand what it means to be a part of God's family. Even our infatuation with the "biological" and "adopted" labels and the distinction between the two shows our tendency to qualify children into categories based around flesh and blood. As long as that's the case, we'll struggle with a gospel that tells the story of a spiritual, transracial adoption that changes the lives of each of us for all eternity. We are adopted into the family of God, and the implications of this are huge for understanding and living out Christianity.

Salvation in Galatians

As we think through what Paul teaches about adoption in Galatians 3:26–4:7, it will be helpful to recap what he has said so far in this letter concerning justification. One statement really sums it up.

We Are Saved by Grace Alone through Faith Alone in Christ Alone

In Galatians 1 we saw that God's pleasure in us is not based on our performance for Him. We're not working to earn God's favor. That's legalism, and it's what Paul is addressing throughout Galatians. Legalism is working in our own power, according to our own rules, to earn God's favor. That's not the gospel.

We also want to avoid hypocrisy, that is, living lives that don't match the gospel we claim to believe. Paul confronts this error in Galatians 2. If we indeed trust and follow Christ, our lives will reflect His teachings as we are more and more conformed to His image.

We are saved through faith alone. God's pleasure in us is based on Christ's performance for us. We trust in Christ, and in so doing, we are accepted by God and alive to Him. As Paul says,

I have been crucified with Christ and I no longer live, but Christ lives in me. The life I now live in the body, I live by faith in the Son of God, who loved me and gave Himself for me. (2:19-20)

We are saved by grace alone through faith alone in Christ alone.

In Galatians 3 Paul covers 2,000 years of Old Testament history, from Abraham through Moses to Christ. We saw that the climax of all history, not only biblical history, but all history, centers around Christ. The promise given to Abraham and the law given to Moses were both given to point us to Christ. Jesus fulfills the law of Moses, and Jesus completes the promise to Abraham. That's why salvation comes only through Christ.

Justification

The main doctrine we've seen in Galatians 1–3 is the doctrine of justification. In Galatians 2 we defined *justification* as the gracious act of God by which He declares a sinner righteous solely through faith in Jesus Christ. This is the doctrine, Luther said, upon which the church stands or falls (Sproul, *Acts*, 266). According to Calvin, it is "the hinge around which everything turns" (ibid., 66).

By grace through faith in Christ **we are right before God the judge**. Our righteousness doesn't have to be earned because Christ has earned it for us. He is our righteousness. Our righteousness is in heaven, and our standing before God is not based on the righteousness we can "work up" every day, but based solely on the righteousness of the One who sits at God's right hand.

Adoption

We cannot over-emphasize the importance of the doctrine of justification, for every follower of Christ needs a strong understanding of this biblical teaching. But justification is not the end of the gospel. In fact, it may not even be the greatest truth in the gospel. Here I want to borrow language from J. I. Packer's excellent book, *Knowing God*:

> [Adoption] is *the highest privilege that the gospel offers*: higher even than justification. This may cause raising of eyebrows, for justification is the gift of God on which since Luther evangelicals have laid the greatest stress, and we are accustomed to say, almost without thinking, that free justification is God's supreme blessing to us sinners.

Nonetheless, careful thought will show the truth of the statement we have just made.

That justification—by which we mean God's forgiveness of the past together with his acceptance for the future—is the *primary and fundamental* blessing of the gospel is not in question. Justification is the *primary* blessing, because it meets our primary spiritual need. We all stand by nature under God's judgment; his law condemns us, guilt gnaws at us, making us restless, miserable, and in our lucid moments afraid; we have no peace in ourselves because we have no peace with our Maker. So we need the forgiveness of our sins, and assurance of a restored relationship with God, more than we need anything else in the world; and this the gospel offers us before it offers us anything else.

. . . But this is not to say that justification is the *highest* blessing of the gospel. Adoption is higher, because of the richer relationship with God that it involves. (Packer, *Knowing God*, 206–7)

Packer goes on to explain why adoption is a higher blessing than justification. The doctrine of justification makes us right before God the judge, but in the doctrine of adoption **we are loved by God the Father**. In justification, the picture is legal; we stand before a judge who makes a pronouncement. But in adoption, the judge not only declares you "Not guilty," but He also gets up off the bench, comes down to where you are, takes your chains off of you, and He says, "Come home with Me as My son." Packer says, "To be right with God the Judge is a great thing, but to be loved and cared for by God the Father is a greater" (ibid.). That's the truth we need to contemplate in this next section of Galatians: the idea that you and I are loved by God the Father. In answer to the question, "What is a Christian?" Packer says, "The richest answer I know is that a Christian is one who has God as Father" (ibid., 200). He continues,

If you want to judge how well a person understands Christianity, find out how much he makes of the thought of being God's child, and having God as his Father. If this is not the thought that prompts and controls his worship and prayers and his whole outlook on life, it means that he does not understand Christianity very well at all. (ibid., 201)

The church should be a people whose worship and prayers and outlook on life are all prompted and controlled by the fact that we are children of God.

The Adoptive Father

Galatians 3:26 is a summary statement of everything we have seen up to this point in Galatians: "For you are all sons of God through faith in Christ Jesus." Notice that Paul doesn't say "sons and daughters" or "children" here—he purposely calls God's people "sons." This is not an attempt to be chauvinistic. Elsewhere God refers to His people as sons and daughters (see Isa 43:6) and children (Ezek 16:21). In light of Galatians 4:1-5 we can see that Paul is actually contrasting "sons" with "children." Understanding the background for these verses is important for seeing the significance of sonship.

There's debate over what Paul is referring to in 4:1-5, whether he's alluding to Jewish, Greek, or Roman customs concerning slaves and guardians. Regardless of which of these cultures is in view, each culture had a time during which a boy, even though he was an heir in the family, would basically be treated like a slave. At a certain age the individual's status would change, and he would take on the responsibilities of manhood. He would officially pass from being a child—like a servant—to a son.

But Paul did not speak of "sons and daughters" in this illustration because inheritance in that day was reserved for sons, not daughters. Still, the Bible is not being chauvinistic here; Paul was actually being very counter-cultural for his day. According to 3:28 the full rights of a son, including the full inheritance, are granted to all who belong to Christ, regardless of whether they are male or female.

Paul takes the illustration of what happens when someone receives the full rights of a son in adoption, and he uses it to describe what God does in our lives by grace through faith in Christ.

There are two actions—radical, glorious actions—God takes to adopt us as sons.

God Sent His Son So That We Might Receive the Position of Sons

Galatians says, "When the time came to completion, God sent His Son, born of a woman, born under the law, to redeem those under the law, so that we might receive adoption as sons" (4:4-5). The word for *adoption* specifically means, "to place someone as an adult son." God adopts us as sons by sending His Son. That leads to the question, What is it about God sending His Son that makes it possible for us to be adopted as His sons? The contemporary analogy of adoption, though it's not precisely the same as adoption in Paul's first-century context, will hopefully help illustrate the Bible's answer to that question.

Consider the following conditions that must be met if you want to adopt a child today.

Adoption requires someone who comes at the right time. Anyone who's been through an adoption process knows the grueling pain of waiting and waiting, getting tons of forms together. You'd think it'd be as easy as connecting an orphan with a willing parent, but there's so much more that goes into it. In the same way, God sending His Son to this earth when He did was not an accident. Paul says that God sent His Son "when the time came to completion" (4:4). This is such a great Christmas text because it points to the significance not only of what happened 2,000 years ago when Jesus was born, but also why it happened at that time. The timing was intentional in every way.

When God sent His Son, **it was the right time theologically**. Everything that was going on in the Old Testament was leading up to this point. The promise to Abraham had been given, the law of Moses had done its work to drive men to anticipate Christ, and over 300 prophecies had been given, all of it aimed toward this time. Christmas didn't just happen. It was the culmination of a plan devised in the eternal counsel of God before the creation of the world (Eph 1:4).

Also, **it was the right time religiously**. The paganism of ancient Rome and the idolatry that pervaded the Roman empire had taken the culture of Jesus' day to new lows. Spiritual hunger was not just evident among the Jewish people who were longing for a Messiah (though they didn't realize what was coming), but a spiritual hunger dominated the Roman cultural landscape as well.

Two other factors indicate that the timing for Christ's coming was right. **It was the right time culturally**. The Greek language had become common and practically universal, thus allowing for the spread of the gospel more easily across the known world.

Finally, **it was the right time politically**. The *Pax Romana*, or Roman peace, prevailed. Rome had conquered and subdued surrounding nations, and as a result it built roads permitting travel and commerce to flourish. It would be much easier to take the gospel to the far corners of the world in such conditions. (On the timing of Christ's coming, see Stott, *Message of Galatians*, 105–6; Ryken, *Galatians*, 160).

When we think of the timing of these events, we shouldn't imagine that God was sitting in heaven thinking, *Things are lining up well; this seems like a good time to send My Son.* No, God in His sovereignty was designing all of history for this moment in time. It was an appointment. Likewise, God has another appointment for Christ's return, and that won't be by accident either. God, in His sovereign design, has ordained a time when Jesus will come back. Revelation 22:20 says, "He who testifies about these things says, 'Yes, I am coming quickly.'"

Adoption requires someone who possesses the right qualifications, in addition to the right timing.[4] In order to go through a contemporary adoption process, you have to go through screenings, fingerprint tests, background studies, and home studies, all in order to fit the qualifications. My wife and I couldn't adopt from one particular country because we weren't old enough, and for a while we couldn't adopt from any country because we didn't have a home due to Hurricane Katrina. There were numerous qualifications we had to meet. In a much deeper way, adoption into God's family requires the right qualifications. For instance, who can pay the price for sinners to be saved? That question points to only one possible person in history: Jesus. And what are His qualifications?

Jesus is fully divine. "God sent His Son," the One Colossians 1:15 says is "the image of the invisible God." Jesus is not just a divine surrogate. He is, in the words of Philippians 2:6, "in the form of God." God did not create His Son; He *sent* His Son, the pre-existent, fully divine, infinite Son of God, who alone can bear the infinite wrath of God.

Jesus is fully human. "God sent His Son," Paul tells us, and He was "born of a woman" (Gal 4:4). Paul makes the same point in the midst of Philippians 2:5-11, a passage that is theologically packed. Here's how the apostle refers to Christ:

> *who, existing in the form of God*
> *did not consider equality with God*
> *as something to be used for His own advantage.*

---

[4] Much of the discussion on Christ's qualifications is taken from Stott, *The Message of Galatians*, 106.

Instead He emptied Himself
by assuming the form of a slave,
taking on the likeness of men.

And when He had come as a man
in His external form, . . . (Phil 2:6-7)

Paul's reference to Christ's "external form" should not be taken to mean that Jesus only appeared to be human. Rather, Paul is referring to the fact that Christ had a physical body like all men. Jesus was both fully divine and fully human.

Christ had a normal birth, complete with a dingy manger and soiled swaddling clothes, as any other poor peasant in Palestine would have had. Luther said Christianity "does not begin at the top, as all other religions do; it begins at the bottom" (Luther, *Lectures on Galatians*, 26:30). He continues,

> you must run directly to the manger and the mother's womb, embrace this Infant and Virgin's Child in your arms, and look at Him—born, being nursed, growing up, going about in human society, teaching, dying, rising again, ascending above all the heavens, and having authority over all things. (ibid.)

Jesus is fully righteous. Not only was He "born of a woman," but also He was "born under the law" (Gal 4:4). Jesus was born not simply a man, but more specifically a Jewish man who grew up in a Jewish home, attending the Jewish synagogue. He perfectly fulfilled all the demands of the law of God. If Jesus had not been righteous, He would not have been able to redeem unrighteous men.

Adoption requires someone who comes at the right time and someone who has the right qualifications. There's one more requirement that should be mentioned:

Adoption requires someone who has the right resolve. You don't adopt accidentally; you adopt purposefully.

Jesus came with a purpose: God sent His Son "to redeem those under law, so that we might receive adoption as sons" (4:5). **He determined to redeem us.** Here's how Paul puts it:

Praise the God and Father of our Lord Jesus Christ, who has blessed us in Christ with every spiritual blessing in the heavens. For He chose us in Him, before the foundation of the world, to be holy and blameless in

His sight. In love He predestined us to be adopted through Jesus Christ for Himself, according to His favor and will. (Eph 1:3-5)

As a parent takes the initiative to seek out and adopt a child, so it was God's pleasure and will before the creation of the world to set His affections on us. But there's a big difference between a contemporary story of earthly adoption and the biblical story of spiritual adoption. Earthly adoption is often glamorized, even over-glamorized, as we think about sweet, precious, innocent children all over the world just waiting to be adopted by a family. But when you look at Ephesians 2, the people who are adopted are objects of wrath who follow the ruler of this world, Satan, gratifying the cravings of their sinful nature (Eph 2:1-3). Russell Moore, himself an adoptive parent, makes the following analogy with respect to the contemporary picture of adoption:

> Imagine for a moment that you're adopting a child. As you meet with the social worker in the last stage of the process, you're told that this 12-year-old has been in and out of psychotherapy since he was three. He persists in burning things, and attempting repeatedly to skin animals alive. He "acts out sexually," the social worker says, although she doesn't really fill you in on what that means. She continues with a little family history. This boy's father, grandfather, great-grandfather, and great-great-grandfather all had histories of violence, ranging from spousal abuse to serial murder. Each of them ended their own lives. Think for a minute. Would you want this child? If you did adopt him, wouldn't you watch nervously as he played with your other children? Would you watch him nervously as he looks at the knife on the kitchen table? Would you leave the room as he watched a movie on TV with your daughter, with the lights out? (Moore, *Adopted for Life*, 29)

Then Moore identifies this potentially problematic 12-year-old: "He's you. And he's me. That's what the Gospel is telling us" (ibid.). Praise God that though there was nothing in us to draw Him to us, God determined to redeem us. And lest that sound like an exaggeration of our evil and sinfulness, look at the cross. Look at the picture of God's wrath against sin. It was no minor offense for which Jesus died.

Jesus determined to redeem us, and **He died to rescue us.** Praise God for His resolve. The other day I was playing with my son whom we adopted from Kazakhstan, and his favorite question now is "Why?" When I told him I loved him, he asked, "Why?" I said, "'Cause you're my son." And, of course, he asked, "Why?" How do you answer that? Out of all the children in all the world, why is *he* my son? I started thinking about all the factors that had to come together, from the timing to the qualifications, to the ups and downs and the days my wife and I wondered if we could do this. I felt the tears well up, though my son didn't even know what was going on (probably sorry that he asked why). I looked at this precious little boy and I said, "Because we wanted you, buddy. And we came to get you. That's why you're my son." In a much greater way, you and I have a God who says, "I love you." And when we ask, "Why, God?" He answers, "Because you're My son." "But why?" "Because I wanted you," He says, "and I came to get you." Praise God that He sent His Son so that we might receive the position of sons.

As great as the reality of being a son is, the gospel could stop there and we would fall to our knees in worship, but there's more good news. The gospel doesn't just declare us "justified," nor does it only give us a new position, a new status. Paul tells us about another blessing: "And because you are sons, God has sent the Spirit of His Son into our hearts, crying, '*Abba*, Father!'" (Gal 4:6).

God Sent His Spirit So That We Might Experience the Privileges of Sonship

Once you adopt a child, he or she takes a new position in the family, but this is not where the story stops. This is where the story really gets good, which is why we can't be satisfied with an I-prayed-a-prayer-however-many-years-ago kind of Christianity. There is so much more! My children know that I'm their father and they're my children, not only because of the love we showed them by traveling to the other side of the world to adopt them, but because of the love I show them today. Their status is based on what a judge in their country declared years ago, but their life is based on our relationship every day as we play cars and read books and run around the yard and go to Moe's for dinner and sing songs on the way home.

So too with God! Your status with Him was settled on the day you were declared righteous through faith in Christ. But there is more here than simply a change in status. You have new life, a living relationship with God in which He communes with you and sustains you on a daily basis with love, affection, and strength. Coming to Christ changes who we are.

We live with a new identity before God. In the words of Galatians 3:27, **we are "baptized into Christ."** This is a picture of immersion into the life of Christ; it's what water baptism symbolizes and signifies. This was huge in context when we remember that Paul was addressing Judaizers—those who were saying that you needed to be circumcised in order to be saved. Paul talks about the picture of baptism, which in certain ways replaced circumcision as the identifying marker of the Christian, though Paul is in no way saying that you must be baptized in order to be saved. Instead, baptism is an outward picture of an inward reality, the reality of experiencing a transforming identification with Christ. Nevertheless, baptism is not just an optional thing to consider: if you are a follower of Christ, this is an extremely important step of obedience as the picture of your identification with Christ. Again, it's not necessary in order to be saved, but it is a fruit of obedience commanded by God.

And as we are baptized into Christ, Paul says **we are clothed with Christ**. Notice the imagery here, for Paul speaks of putting on Christ "like a garment" (3:27). In Old Testament culture, when you passed from childhood into manhood and received your full rights as a son, you would literally put on different clothes. Likewise, our old self in Adam is removed and discarded when we become new by faith in Christ. This is what happens when we are united to Him.

Not only are believers united *to* Christ, but also **we are united *in* Christ**. In verse 28 Paul starts listing some of the barriers that separated people in the first century, and these are barriers that still separate people today. He starts with ethnic or racial barriers, Jews and Greeks. Then he moves to social barriers, slave or free. Finally, Paul talks about the gender barriers of male and female. Paul is not saying that when you come to Christ you lose these distinctions, that you're no longer a Jew or a Greek, slave or free, male or female. Instead, he's saying that these barriers no longer divide because we are all one in Christ Jesus. Oh, this is the beauty of the church summed up in one verse: a people united not by their ethnicity, their socioeconomic status or gender, not by this or that artificial distinction set up in a particular culture or society, but a people from all ethnicities, socioeconomic statuses, and genders united together as one in Christ. We all stand before God the same, needing Christ, dependent on Christ, not one of us better or worse. All of us need grace, and we find it in Christ alone, through whom we have all become sons of God!

Experiencing unity in Christ is one of the great joys of traveling to other countries and meeting with believers there. For instance, when you sit down with Christians in India, there are so many differences that would separate you: you eat differently, you speak different languages, you have different political viewpoints, and you approach life differently. Yet, you immediately have a bond in Christ, and it's a beautiful bond that transcends any differences. It's not a socially, politically, or economically manufactured unity; rather, it's a unity that comes from each person being in Christ. Union with Christ automatically establishes communion with other Christians.

Finally, in addition to being baptized into Christ, clothed with Christ, and united in Christ, **we each belong to Christ**. In 3:29 Paul says, "And if you belong to Christ, then you are Abraham's seed." Here Paul takes this unity and ties it to the Old Testament line of saints. We belong to Abraham, Isaac, Jacob, Moses, Joshua, Samuel, David, Solomon, Isaiah, and Jeremiah. We all belong to Christ.

We saw previously that because we've been adopted, we live with a new identity before God. There is a second blessing we should mention.

We enjoy intimacy with God. The Spirit transforms not only our identity, but also our intimacy with God. Paul says, "And because you are sons, God has sent the Spirit of His Son into our hearts, crying, '*Abba*, Father!'" (4:6). Remember the context of what Paul has developed up to this point. At the end of chapter 3 and into the beginning of chapter 4, Paul built the case that **we were once held captive by God's law**. Apart from Christ, we were held prisoners by the law, locked up in our sin (3:23). The commands of God condemned us because we could not keep them. Paul says, "In the same way we also, when we were children, were in slavery under the elemental forces of the world" (4:3). We were held captive by the law; but now, everything has changed.

Though we were previously imprisoned by the law God gave as a result of sin, **now we're captivated by His love**. Our situation under the new covenant in Christ is much different from the situation of believers under the old covenant. Consider the fear and trembling associated with the giving of the law in Exodus 19:9-22. The people were warned, "Anyone who touches the mountain will be put to death" (v. 12). In the morning, "there was thunder and lightning, a thick cloud on the mountain, and a loud trumpet sound, so that all the people in the camp shuddered" (v. 16). The mountain was "completely enveloped in smoke" and it "shook violently" (v. 18). After that encounter, the people begged

Moses, "You speak to us, and we will listen, . . . but don't let God speak to us, or we will die" (Exod 20:19).

This is a picture of the effect of the law. The law revealed man's sin and separation from God, such that in the Old Testament, men trembled at the thought of being anywhere near God. Now take that image and bring it into the New Testament, specifically to the picture of adoption in Galatians 3–4. The people of God were awed and frightened at the prospect of approaching God under the law in the Old Testament, and rightfully so; yet this is the privilege of every single person who is united to Christ. You and I approach God, the same God of Exodus 19, and we do so with "boldness and confident access through faith in Him" (Eph 3:12). And not only do we have confidence, but we also have intimacy: we cry out, "*Abba*, Father" (Gal 4:6).

This word *Abba* is sometimes misunderstood and over-sentimentalized as a word that simply means "Daddy," which gives the impression that this is almost like baby talk. But that's not how Scripture uses this title for God. This is a groaning, a longing for a father. It's Jesus in the garden, crying out (Mark 14:36). Likewise, the same Spirit in us cries out, "*Abba*, Father" (Rom 8:15). It's my son, when he's scared, and he grabs on tight to my neck, and he cries out, "Daddy!" It's when you hear the news you feared, you get the diagnosis you dreaded most, you experience the circumstances you never could have imagined happening, and you fall on your knees and cry out, "*Abba*, Father!" For even in those moments, you do not have a spirit that makes you a slave again to fear (Rom 8:15). No matter what this world brings, you have nothing to fear because you have received the spirit of sonship, leading us to cry out, "*Abba*, Father!"

Do we realize that the privilege of approaching God, which was once reserved only for Moses in the Old Testament, is now what happens when you do something as simple as bowing your head before a meal? It's good to be a son, to enjoy intimacy with God. And the Judaizers were missing it, just as many professing Christians today are missing it. They've got the religious routine down, but they have no intimacy with God.

The conversion of the well-known eighteenth-century evangelist John Wesley is a perfect example. Wesley was an honor graduate of Oxford University, an ordained clergyman in the Church of England, and orthodox in his theology. He was active in practical good works, regularly visiting the inmates of prisons and workhouses in London and helping distribute food and clothing to slum children and orphans. He studied the Bible diligently and attended numerous Sunday services as well as various other services during the week. He generously gave offerings to the church and alms to the poor. He prayed and fasted and lived an exemplary moral life. He even spent several years as a missionary to American Indians in what was then the British colony of Georgia. Yet upon returning to England he confessed in his journal, "I who went to America to convert others was never myself converted to God." Later reflecting on his preconversion condition, he said, "I had even then the faith of a *servant*, though not that of a son" (Stott, *Message of Galatians*, 109).

Are you a son? I'm not asking whether you go to church, read your Bible, or raise your kids a certain way. But do you have intimacy with God as Father? This is what it means to be a son.

Finally, we are guaranteed an inheritance from God. The argument keeps building: you are no longer a slave, Paul says, but a son, and because you are a son, you receive the inheritance. Our salvation and the gospel become more beautiful as you dive deeper into them. We've gone from justification, which means being right before God the judge; to becoming sons, which means we have a new identity and enjoy a new intimacy; and now, since we are sons, God has also made us heirs.

We have been adopted, and the blessings we receive are staggering. Three blessings in particular are worth mentioning. First, **we have an eternal Father.** Some people have never really had a father in their lives, while others have had great fathers who have pointed to a heavenly Father. But even the best earthly father is an inadequate picture of God as our Father and of our spiritual adoption. For example, some say that children who were adopted have a more difficult time with their identity in a family. I want to be a good father to my children, for them to know every day that they are fully in my family and that I am here to stay as their father. I want them to be secure in my love. On a much grander scale, this is what God does in adoption. He assures us of His love. Even when we fall, He is our Father. This is good news for those who have fallen prey to sin. Like any good father, God may discipline us, but He will do it because He has deep love and affection for us.

Second, our adoption by God means that **we have an eternal family.** We've already seen in 3:28 that in Christ we have union with one another. As those in God's family, we relate to one another as brothers and sisters. Amazingly, Romans 8:17 says that we are "coheirs with Christ," and elsewhere we are told that we are brothers with Jesus (Heb 2:11). He is our elder brother, though not in a way that compromises His divinity, as some cults believe. We are not equal to Jesus. But Scripture does teach that everything that belongs to Jesus belongs to us as coheirs. Now that's good news *and* bad news. It's bad news because Jesus suffered, and the world hated Him. Therefore, being in the family with Jesus may cost us our lives. But it's also good news because if we share in His sufferings, we will also share in His glory (Rom 8:17). Together, we will enjoy all that Christ has for all of eternity. This is a good family, one that you *want* to be adopted into.

Third, in addition to having an eternal Father and an eternal family, **we have an eternal home**. When you're brought into a new home and the adoption is complete, it's not temporary.

Nobody's coming to my house from Kazakhstan or China to take my children away—nobody. You and I can have the same firm confidence based on the authority of God's Word that we will always belong to Him. God has sent His Son into the world that we might receive the position of sons. And when we trust in Christ for salvation, God takes us into His home as heirs, and nobody's taking us away—nobody.

Isn't it indescribably glorious to be adopted by God?

Reflect and Discuss

1. What's the difference between being justified and being adopted?
2. What does the timing of Christ's coming teach you about God's providence in the world and in redemption? Did Jesus come at just the right time? Explain.
3. Could anyone other than Jesus have reconciled us to God? Explain your answer.
4. How might seeing one's fundamental identity as biological undermine the gospel? Why would this have been a strong temptation for Jews in Paul's day?
5. Identify the problem with the following statement: "God adopts us because we deserve a better life."
6. How should the new identity of a follower of Christ affect his or her battle with sin? What about fear? Covetousness? Divisiveness? Why should the doctrine of adoption inspire greater prayer and deeper worship?
7. How would you respond to someone who said that God is the Father of everyone, regardless of their faith?

8. Does intimacy with God as your Father naturally lead to a low or irreverent view of God? Explain.
9. How should the doctrine of adoption impact the way we view others in the church? Do you think most people in your church view the church as a family, an event, or a building? Why?
10. Paul speaks of the inheritance believers receive by virtue of their adoption. List some of these privileges.

Free to Grow

GALATIANS 4:8-31

Main Idea: Although we may encounter opposition from those who claim to be religious, we must walk in God's grace and live with great zeal for His purpose.

Three Prayers

I. **God, Show Us How to Walk in Your Grace (4:8-11,21-31).**
    A. Show us how we got here.
    B. Show us who we are.
    C. Show us where we're going.

II. **God, Help Us to Trust in Your Word (4:12-16).**
    A. Help us to live it when it's not easy.
    B. Help us to hear it when it's not popular.

III. **God, Give Us Great Zeal for Your Purpose (4:17-20).**
    A. Give us a passion to be conformed to the image of Christ.
    B. Give us a passion to see others transformed for the glory of Christ.

While Galatians 4:8-31 is a complicated text, it gives us a glimpse into Paul the pastor like few other texts do. Up to this point, Paul has been very confrontational with the church at Galatia, calling them "foolish" (3:1,3) and confronting them about major issues related to the gospel. Paul has shown us that there's a time for that—for really calling the church out when they are missing God's Word. But now, after a tough three and a half chapters, Paul gives us some of the strongest words of personal affection that we see anywhere in his writings. Luther said that these words "breathe Paul's own tears" (Luther, *Lectures on Galatians*, 27:299).

This text in many ways sums up my gratitude and care for the church I pastor. I long for it to be conformed to the image of Christ. Based on this text, three prayers arise that are appropriate for any church desiring to follow Christ faithfully. However, like other texts in Galatians, these verses are complicated and need some unpacking. By God's grace and with the leadership of His Spirit, that's what we'll seek to do.

Three times in this passage Paul calls the Galatians "brothers" (4:12,28,31), and then in verse 19 he calls them "children." Paul's affection for them is evident. Three prayers are prompted as we get a glimpse of Paul's pastoral heart.

God, Show Us How to Walk in Your Grace
GALATIANS 4:8-11,21-31

In many senses, Paul is not introducing new information in Galatians 4. Instead, he's still recapping what he has been talking about throughout chapter 3 (and even before that). In 4:8-11 and then again in the passage about Sarah and Hagar in 4:21-31, Paul returns to the image of slavery, reminding the Galatians yet again about the transformation that has taken place in their lives. They have gone from slavery to sonship. Like the Galatians, we need to pray that God would make us aware of what He has done for us in Christ so that we, in turn, will live accordingly.

Show Us How We Got Here

We can summarize Paul's argument in this passage by looking through three different lenses: how we got here, who we are, and where we're going. First we'll look at how we got here. Paul's discussion of slavery, particularly in relation to the law, is well illustrated at the end of chapter 4 by the analogy of Sarah and Hagar.

This final section in 4:21-31 serves as a closing summation of chapters 3 and 4. Paul takes us all the way back to Genesis 16–17 where we're introduced to Hagar, a slave woman in Abraham's household. Abraham and his wife, Sarah, were worried that they were not going to have an heir to carry on their line, so Sarah suggested that Abraham build his family through Hagar. This is a classic example of the not-so-pretty-side of the Old Testament, as Abraham then had a child through Hagar. That child's name was Ishmael. Abraham thought that if God was going to bless his line, He'd apparently do it through Ishmael, who was basically a slave in Abraham's household. But God corrected Abraham and told him that he would have a son with Sarah and that they were to name him Isaac. Isaac would be the child that God had promised, and God would make this happen miraculously, when Abraham was 100 and Sarah was 90 years old.

Paul uses this story as an illustration to contrast the child born into slavery, Ishmael, and the child born from the promise, Isaac. He also contrasts the mothers, Hagar as a slave woman and Sarah as a free woman. Paul says Hagar and Ishmael stand for the old covenant, the law, which produced slaves. This is exactly what Paul talked about in Galatians 3, that we are imprisoned by the law (3:23). But, Paul says, we have been set free (3:25). We do not become children of God by the law, by the old covenant, but by the promise of God, by the new covenant. To put it another way, we are not saved by obedience to the law, but by faith in the promise of God.

With the illustration of Sarah and Hagar in 4:21-31, as well as the mention of our slavery to sin in 4:8-11, Paul is saying exactly what he's been saying throughout Galatians: **we've not been obedient to the law**. The old covenant was given at Mount Sinai and required God's people to keep the law (see Exod 19–20). But we have all disobeyed the law, which means salvation can't come through the law. So how does salvation come? It comes because **we've been awakened by the Spirit**. The key phrase is in 4:29, where it says that Isaac was "born according to the Spirit." This was the difference between Isaac and Ishmael: Ishmael was born according to the flesh, that is, in the natural way that children are born. Abraham and Hagar attempted to produce an heir through their own human ability, since Sarah couldn't have children. But Isaac was born supernaturally, in the sense that this was something that could only happen if God intervened with a miracle between a 100-year-old man and a 90-year-old woman. This illustration takes us all the way back to 3:2, where Paul asked the Galatians, "Did you receive the Spirit by the works of the law or by hearing with faith?" Paul is telling us that our status as sons, as children of faith in God's promise, comes about by the Spirit and not by natural human effort.

Show Us Who We Are

We now turn to Paul's discussion of who we are. As a result of being awakened by the Spirit, **we are not slaves to religion**. Paul is once again reiterating in this passage that we are no longer slaves. That's the whole point of the illustration with Hagar and Sarah, namely, that we are to get rid of the slave woman and her son (4:30). We're not slaves to the law anymore. We're children of freedom. We're not saved by obeying the law in addition to trusting in Christ for salvation, which is exactly what the Galatians had started thinking as a result of the Judaizers. Paul describes the situation of the Galatians in 4:8-11.

In verse 8 Paul says that the Galatians were slaves to those who are not gods, a reference to false gods or demons. Remember that most of the Galatian Christians were not formerly Jewish, but rather pagan. Therefore, Paul essentially reminds them that they used to worship pagan gods. Then, in verse 9, he says that they are turning back to slavery. And to what are they turning back? The apostle gets specific in verse 10, saying that their slavery is shown in their observance of "special days, months, seasons, and years," a general reference to a broad range of Jewish festivals, events, and celebrations.

What Paul says here is astonishing. He tells the Galatians that they used to be pagans who worshiped demons, but then they were set free by the gospel. Now they're turning to Jewish holy days and festivals, giving themselves to slavery and paganism again. Did you catch that? Paul is talking about those who celebrate these Jewish holy days and festivals as a way to get to God, and he is equating their ceremonies with the same pagan religious practices the Galatians participated in before they came to Christ. In other words, Paul refers to these Jewish ordinances as demonic when they're approached as ways to make oneself right before God. This is the exact same thing pagans are doing in their religions.

Let me put this into contemporary language: if you go to church, sing songs, and study the Word, thinking this is how you're going to work to earn God's favor, then you are no different from the over one billion Hindus in the world today who are bowing down to their gods. If your Christianity is a check-off box in order to make you feel good about yourself before God, in order to save your skin on the day of judgment, then your Christianity is no different from every other religion in the world, and ultimately it will condemn you. Paul is uncovering a scheme of the Devil in the first century that continues in the twenty-first century. It is subtly and dangerously deceiving. What if Satan's strategy to condemn your soul involves not tempting you to do all the wrong things, but instead leading you to do all the right things with the wrong spirit? What if Satan actually wants you to come to church, lead a small group, teach, and lead your home in an upright way? What if he's in favor of you doing all those things, just so long as you think that by doing those things you're working your way to God?

- You say, "Well, I pray." Big deal, Muslims pray.
- You say, "Well, I go to worship." Big deal, Hindus go to worship. They worship all day long.

- You say, "Well, I study the Bible." So do Jehovah's Witnesses, and they can quote it better than most Christians.
- You say, "Well, I go on mission trips." So do Mormons—scores of them give years of their lives to do so.

If your Christianity consists of slavery to religion in order to make yourself right before God, then it's just as if you're giving yourself to the pagan religions of the world. But Christianity is radically different from those worldly religions. Rather than slaves of religion, **we are sons in a relationship with God**. Paul says that the Galatians know God, and then he pauses and says, "or rather have become known by God" (v. 9). To use the language of 4:1-7, we are sons of God. Why would we live like a slave to religion when we are sons in a relationship with God? God knows us intimately, and the idea here is of deep, personal knowledge. We know God, and He knows us!

I am so thankful for the intimate relationship I have with my wife. When an anniversary comes up and I try to think of a way for us to celebrate, I don't come up with a list of things I need to do to make my wife happy. No, it isn't about checking off boxes. I think about how much I love her and how much I want to honor her and give to her and bless her. Why? Because I know her, and she knows me.

We ought to view our relationship with God similarly. We can either make Christianity just like every other world religion and check off our boxes every week and go through the routine and the ritual, or we can step into the intimate presence of God. We ought not be a people who prayed a prayer a while ago and now are just trying to do our best to get things right with our lives on a week-in and week-out basis. We should be a people who walk with God and know Him intimately. We ought to serve God wholeheartedly, not because we're trying to make ourselves right, but because we've been made right by God's grace. We walk with Him as sons who know Him and love Him and enjoy Him and glorify Him, no matter what it costs us.

Show Us Where We're Going

Having seen how we got here and who we are, Paul also wants us to know **where we're going**. In 4:25 Paul talks about how Hagar corresponds to the earthly city of Jerusalem, which symbolizes slavery. But there is freedom in the heavenly Jerusalem, in being a child of promise living for the Jerusalem that is above (v. 26). And Paul reminds us that because we are free, **we are not living for earthly pleasure**. We aren't in slavery to the weak and miserable principles of the world. Instead, **we are living for a heavenly home**. We're free people who are no longer in bondage to this world. We don't live like everybody else, nor do we live for what everybody else lives for. We're sons who live for a Father who is preparing a place for us in a heavenly home, and this changes everything about our lives in this world. May God show us how to walk in His grace.

We have been saved by grace; that much is clear. But Paul's burden for the church at Galatia is for them to realize what it means to live by that grace—not as slaves to religion, but as sons in a relationship to God; and not for earthly pleasure, but for a heavenly home. For many of us, there is so much room to grow in this area.

So the first prayer in this passage is that God would show us how to walk in His grace. Here is the second.

God, Help Us to Trust in Your Word
GALATIANS 4:12-16

We've taken verses 8-11 and 21-31 somewhat like bookends on this section of Galatians 4. Now we need to look in between at verses 12-20. Paul commends the Galatian believers in verses 12-16.

In verse 12 Paul talks about how he became like the Galatians in order to lead them to Christ. In other words, Paul, a Jewish man, when he went into Gentile contexts, didn't follow all of his Jewish customs. Instead, he put them aside in order to show that salvation was not dependent on these things. Now he's pleading with the Galatians to do the same—to stop living like they needed to do certain things in the law in order to be saved.

In verses 13-14 Paul talks about how he first met the Galatians. The apostle was sick. Some scholars think he had malaria, others have suggested other illnesses, but whatever Paul's issue was, it was apparently pretty bad, almost repulsive. Yet the Christians there had accepted him, even when it wasn't easy to do so. And they did so with joy, verse 15 says, even sacrificing themselves for his sake. But apparently they seemed to be almost rejecting Paul now, turning their backs on him, treating him as an enemy (v. 16). This made Paul perplexed, confused, and in a sense, heartbroken.

Help Us to Live It When It's Not Easy

Paul's trials remind us that we need God to help us trust in His Word. By that I mean God must help us to live it when it's not easy. What Paul was asking these Galatians to do—to leave behind Jewish customs and rules—was not easy, particularly when there were teachers in the church saying these customs and rules were necessary for salvation. This was not easy at all, which is probably why Paul implies in verse 12 that living and preaching like this wasn't easy for him. For instance, Paul was ostracized in many ways for reaching out to Gentiles like he did. He was ostracized first of all by the Jewish establishment for coming to Christ, for leaving Judaism to follow what they perceived of basically as a cult. And then after he became a Christian and a part of the church, he was ostracized by Jewish Christians for reaching out to Gentile Christians. It wasn't easy to convert to Christianity in the first century, particularly if you had to leave Jewish customs and rules embedded in an old covenant in order to be a part of a new covenant. In verse 29 Paul gives the example of Ishmael persecuting Isaac to make this very point. This is what happens when you walk by grace and live according to the Word by faith. You will be persecuted.

Interestingly, persecution comes not only from the world, but also from the religious establishment around you. This is a theme that runs throughout the Bible. The prophets were persecuted, and who was it that persecuted them? Was it the surrounding Gentile nations? No, it was the ruling Jewish establishment. Jesus was persecuted, and by whom? By the Pharisees and religious leaders of the day who instigated His execution. In a similar way, Paul was persecuted by these Judaizers. What's the common theme? When you start to live radically by grace, it will cost you. Sure, it will cost you in the outside world, but you'll receive the most trouble from the religious world around you. Throughout the history of God's people, some of the greatest struggles have not come from the outside, but from the inside. This continues to be true today: when people start to really trust in God's Word, when people start taking it at face value and believing it and living it, then there will be religious people who will rise up and make some noise. You will be resisted by the religious establishment when you start to live out the Word. You may even be ostracized, discounted, and labeled a fanatic. The question for us is, Will we live according to God's Word even when it's not easy? For this we need God's help.

Help Us to Hear It When It's Not Popular

Not only do we need God to help us to live out the truth when it's not easy, but we also need God to help us to hear it when it's not popular. Paul closes out verse 16 by saying, "Have I now become your enemy by telling you the truth?" This is what I love about Paul. He has said some hard things to the Galatians, not because he hates them, but because he loves them. Paul was willing to risk his own reputation with the Galatians by telling them the truth instead of telling them what they wanted to hear. This is a good reminder for me or any teacher of the Bible. People love a preacher or a teacher who says just what they want to hear. You can draw the crowds, gain the accolades, and have everything go smoothly as long as you tell people what they want to hear. But when you tell the truth, people will look at you like you're their enemy. So the question for every Bible teacher and preacher is this: Do you (or I) want to be popular or do we want to be faithful? I want to be faithful to God's Word more than I want to be pleasing in people's opinion. As long as God's Word is guiding us, let's ask God to help us hear it and receive it, even when it's not popular.

In verse 17 Paul talks about the strategy of the Judaizers. They sounded like they cared for these believers, but in fact they did not care. Actually, they are leading the Galatians down a road that leads to hell. The Galatians don't want to hear Paul when he tells them their "friends" are wicked; on the contrary, they suspect Paul's motives. Therefore, Paul pleads with the Galatians not to see him as their enemy, telling them of his love. He wanted them to hear and receive the truth and reject the harmful lies. We too must be faithful to the Word, even when it exposes blind spots and areas of our lives that need radical adjustment. Even when it contains truths that you, or frankly I, may not want to hear.

God, Give Us Great Zeal for Your Purpose
GALATIANS 4:17-20

We come now to verses 17-20 in this passage. In verse 18 Paul says that it's good to have zeal—we need to be zealous—as long as it's for the right purpose. Then in verse 19 Paul talks about what he's zealous for. He brings in the imagery of giving birth, saying, "I am again suffering labor pains for you until Christ is formed in you" (v. 19).

Give Us a Passion to Be Conformed to the Image of Christ

Based on this verse, we pray that God would give us a passion to be conformed to the image of Christ. The key word here is "formed" (*morphoo*), which refers to shaping us. More than anything, Paul wanted Christ used as a mold to shape the lives of the Galatians. Paul wants them to be like Christ. We're reminded of Paul's words in 2:20, where he speaks of Christ living in him. Similarly, in 2 Corinthians 4:10 Paul speaks of the purpose of the sufferings of the apostles: "so that the life of Jesus may also be revealed in our body." This is the freedom that Paul is talking about—Christ shaping us, molding us, changing us, and forming us into His image so that we might be liberated to experience life in Him, for Him, through Him, by Him, and with Him. This is my prayer for the church I pastor, that Christ would be formed in them.

Give Us a Passion to See Others Transformed for the Glory of Christ

When Christ is formed in us, which only happens by the Word, this affects our proclamation. So we pray that God would give us a passion to see others transformed for the glory of Christ. We hear Paul's heart at this point. According to Galatians 4:19, this is what he labors and experiences pain for, what he wants more than anything else. Like a mother who longs, even through pain, to give birth to a child, Paul longed to see the Galatians transformed for the glory of Christ. This ought to be the heart of every pastor and also of every follower of Christ. We should pray for each other, teach each other, and model the Christ-life before each other because we want others to be transformed. We are not followers of Christ merely for our own sake. We are here together, for each other. Our churches ought to be communities that weep with each other, plead with each other, confront each other when necessary, pray with each other, and exhort each other. And we do all of this because we want to see each other transformed, not into our own image or some pre-fabricated image of what our culture says we should look like, but instead into the image of Christ. Paul says that he will not be satisfied until that happens. May God help us to be a people who are not satisfied until Christ is formed in us, until we take on the shape of Christ.

Reflect and Discuss

1. In what sense does the gospel bring freedom from slavery? What does it mean to live as a child in a relationship not enslaved to religion?
2. What does it mean to be "known by God" (v. 9)? Why is this an amazing thing to say?
3. What might it look like to rely on the law for salvation? How is this contrary to the gospel?
4. How does Isaac's miraculous birth picture a believer's birth by the Holy Spirit? How are we miracle children (vv. 21-31)?
5. If God still expects His people to obey, how is a relationship with Him different from being a slave to religion?
6. How is any attempt to earn favor before God, even under the banner of religion, a form of paganism?
7. What are some practical ways to grow in an intimate relationship with God?
8. Have you ever become someone's enemy by telling the truth (4:16)? Do you need to speak the truth in love to someone right now? If so, explain why.
9. Why does the truth of the gospel often meet opposition from those who claim to be religious?
10. In verse 19 we see Paul's passion for the spiritual growth of the church in Galatia. In what ways can you foster that kind of love for fellow believers?

Christ Our Liberator

GALATIANS 5:1-15

Main Idea: Paul urges his readers to resist the dangerous message of bondage and encourages them to live in the freedom of Christ.

I. **Christ Has Set Us Free: Live Free (5:1)!**
II. **Christ Has Set Us Free: Live in the Truth (5:2-12).**
   A. A false message
   B. False messengers
III. **Christ Has Set Us Free: Live to Love and Serve (5:13-15).**

Do you enjoy running? I have been running for the past few years, but before this I had no desire to run. I played sports all my life, including four years of baseball in college, but I never enjoyed running without a ball. It was more like punishment than pleasure. Running is what we did in fall conditioning, or what we did when we played terribly. One reason I like baseball is that you can run 90 feet and then stop! So, I have only been in two races in the last 10 years. One of them happened in New Orleans. I weighed about 40 more pounds than I do now. I did not impress anyone. In fact, a lady pushing a stroller passed me! The other race was better. I managed to come in third place. Of course, it was a 1K with first graders but I was pleased with my performance. It was fascinating watching first graders run a race. Most of them sprinted from the starting line, but about a hundred feet later, they tanked. They were walking to the finish line.

Those kids were sort of like the Galatians. Paul illustrates their failure to go the distance: "You were running well. Who prevented you from obeying the truth?" (v. 7). The Galatians started out terrifically but were not persevering to the end. The author of Hebrews also compares the Christian life to a race. He urges readers to "run with endurance the race that lies before us" (Heb 12:1). He also notes that "weight" and "sin" can hinder us from finishing the race. What else can keep us from enduring? Galatians shows us: false teaching.

The Galatians failed to understand how you live the Christian life once you begin it. Particularly, they failed to understand *Christian freedom.* They were not living as freed captives, but as slaves. This happened because they were listening to false teachers.

Let us look at this freedom that Jesus has brought us. Notice three instructions for running/living in the freedom of Christ.

Christ Has Set Us Free: Live Free!
GALATIANS 5:1

Paul begins by saying, "Christ has liberated us to be free. Stand firm then and don't submit again to a yoke of slavery." "If Galatians is the Magna Carta of Christian liberty, then Gal 5:1 has reason to be considered one of the key verses of the epistle" (George, *Galatians* 352). Indeed, this is one of the key verses in the book.

Paul wants his readers to live free. Christ has saved them "to be free," and in that freedom they are called to live. This sentence functions as a transition verse between the last section and what follows. Paul just discussed freedom (3:1–4:31). He calls them out for living as slaves, not as sons (4:7). They were reverting to slavery to idols, the law, and elemental forces (4:1-3,8). Paul illustrated this idea with Isaac and Ishmael to teach that Christians are children of the free, children of promise, walking miracles, born of the Spirit, not children of slavery (4:21-31). In light of all this Paul says, Do not submit to slavery! What follows this exhortation is more on the subject. Before we see it, notice the end of this section in 5:13: "For you were called to be free, brothers."

Because "Christ has liberated us to be free," rest and rejoice in Him. We should rejoice in Christ because we have come to our final resting place. We are not under condemnation, and we do not have to be enslaved to idols.

The exodus is a beautiful picture of how Christ has delivered us. Jesus liberated us not from Egypt, but from sin's awful slavery, and He has brought us into His kingdom. Jesus said, "If the Son sets you free, you really will be free" (John 8:36). If you know this but are not glorifying Christ deeply because of it, then it raises the question, Why not? One of the answers has to be that you have forgotten how terrible slavery was. The gospel is not awesome unless you see the awfulness of your previous condition. Thomas Watson said it well: "Till sin be bitter, Christ will not be sweet" (*The Doctrine of Repentance*, 63).

We need to understand what Christ has done in order to adore Him and not return to slavery. To understand freedom, think about it like this: as believers, we are freed *objectively* (technically, legally) from the guilt of sin, but we struggle to be free *subjectively* (experientially, daily) from the grip of sin. Tim Keller says,

> The whole book of Galatians is about people who, from what we can tell, were objectively freed from guilt (i.e., they seem to have really believed in Jesus), but were going back into a form of works-righteousness. Why? This is a bit of a speculation, but as a pastor over the years and as a human being, I think that deep down inside—maybe it's because of the image of God— everyone knows that he or she should be perfect. We all know that we should be perfect. ("Getting Out")

Objectively we know this: "Therefore, no condemnation now exists for those in Christ Jesus, because the Spirit's law of life in Christ Jesus has set you free from the law of sin and of death" (Rom 8:1). We are free from the *penalty* of sin ("justification"). We do not have to live with a sense of being unacceptable to God. Christ has made us acceptable. Christ alone is perfect, and we must rest in His perfect work performed on our behalf. We must not revert to works-based righteousness.

Subjectively, or experientially, we need to learn how to live free from the *power* of sin ("sanctification"). Gerhard Forde said, "Sanctification is thus simply the art of getting used to justification" (*Christian Spirituality*, 13). We are free, but we do not always live free. We are in need of becoming what we already are. That is sanctification, living as a free, justified person, resting in Christ alone.

We wrestle with our old idols that continue to tempt. We wrestle with the guilt of the law, which tries to condemn us. But we have to thus keep coming back to the gospel and "get used to our justification." Christ has made us righteous.

Questions: Do you believe you are free objectively from condemnation? Do you believe you are accepted in Christ perfectly? Subjectively, are you living out of that new identity, and not reverting to idols or slavery to religion? Objectively, the Galatians were not walking in this truth. They believed that they needed to contribute to their final salvation. They were basically practicing self-atonement by believing that the gospel was "Jesus + something else" (see Tchividjian, *Jesus + Nothing = Everything*). The good news is that you stand accepted today in Christ. Nothing we can do will make us more or less accepted by Him, if we are in Christ. Here is liberty!

Paul opened this book with a statement about freedom. He said that Christ "gave Himself for our sins to rescue us from this present evil age" (1:4). He came to deliver us from the grip of this age: the flesh, elemental spirits, idolatry, and the evil one. Just as Israel got out of Egypt objectively but had slavishness in their hearts, so we too wrestle with believing and living in our freedom. When this happens, we take our eyes off of Christ and our worship is hindered. And when we stop adoring Christ, our Redeemer, we will not grow spiritually. Growth happens as we continue to focus on the glory of Christ, who has made us righteous (2 Cor 3:18).

Keller is so helpful again:

> Years ago when I was trying to understand this, I read sermons by David Martyn Lloyd-Jones on Romans 6, and a particular illustration was illuminating. Imagine, Lloyd-Jones said, that you were a slave in the Southern United States before the Emancipation Proclamation. That means that you couldn't vote; you had no power, and somebody could beat you up and probably kill you. You didn't have rights. So if you were in town and some white person told you to do this or that and was abusive to you, you were very frightened and did anything he said. Now it's ten years later, and the Emancipation Proclamation has been issued. You have rights. But you walk into town, and a white person starts to yell at you. Even though you know with your head, "Hey, I have some rights here," you're still scared and acting like a slave.
>
> That actually is the condition of every Christian. You know, but you don't know. You know that you've been saved from slavery to sin and that you should be free. If you really believed in your heart what you know with your head (i.e., that there is no condemnation for you because you are in Christ Jesus, and God regards you as perfect because of Christ's righteousness), then you would not still be a slave in your heart to success or to what other people think of you. Technically and objectively, you're *not a slave. But God has freed you from sins that you are still enslaved to.* ("Getting Out")

God has freed you from things to which you are still enslaved. You have to work the gospel down deep in order to run in the freedom that is yours.

Because Christ has set us free, "Stand Firm!" Paul says that standing firm in freedom will safeguard us against submitting to legal bondage. Down in Galatians 5:13 he adds that it will safeguard us against danger from the opposite direction; namely, the abuse of freedom or indulging the flesh. He is saying, "Keep it between the guard rails."

In 5:1, he adds, "Don't submit again to a yoke of slavery." He says, do not put on this yoke. This "yoke" probably refers to false teaching that is saying they are not free and that they need to keep the law. To submit to circumcision and adopt the Old Testament law as a means of salvation is slavery. They effectively put themselves in Ishmael's family instead of Isaac's family.

The gospel frees us from condemnation. So do not put on that yoke that says you are not free in Christ. A real test for a teacher is whether or not he or she teaches like a Pharisee or like Paul. Jesus said that the Pharisees tie up "heavy loads" with their list of rules, putting a yoke on the hearers (Matt 23:4). That teaching crushes people. It is lifeless. It offers no hope and no security. Paul, on the other hand, takes people to Christ as their final resting place. In Christ, we find our peace, liberty, joy, and security.

If you are a mother, are you taking your kid to Mount Sinai's laws and leaving him there? Or are you taking him from there and going to Calvary for grace? Let us point our children to the Liberator and Redeemer. The default mode of the heart is self-justification. Every child is a Pharisee in the making. We must teach them the gospel, which is counter-intuitive. Say, "You can't, but Jesus did!" Give them grace. Give them Galatians.

Some think that if you teach freedom in Christ, no one will want to serve Him, but that is not true. The opposite actually happens. When you recognize that Christ has done it all and you truly work this into your heart, you will adore Christ. And an adoring heart does not lead to a sinful life, but a holy life.

My friend Tullian offers a great illustration of such freedom:

> I close my book *Surprised by Grace* with a story (not sure if this really happened or is simply parabolic) from Civil War days before America's slaves were freed, about a northerner who went to a slave auction and purchased a young slave girl. As they walked away from the auction, the man turned to the girl and told her, "You're free."

With amazement she responded, "You mean, I'm free to do whatever I want?"

"Yes," he said.

"And to say whatever I want to say?"

"Yes, anything."

"And to be whatever I want to be?"

"Yep."

"And even go wherever I want to go?"

"Yes," he answered with a smile. "You're free to go wherever you'd like."

She looked at him intently and said, "Then I will go with you." ("Then I Will Go with You")

Tullian comments,

> Some fear that grace-delivered, blood-bought, radical freedom will result in loveless license. But as the above story illustrates, redeeming unconditional love alone (not fear, not guilt, not shame) carries the power to compel heart-felt loyalty to the One who bought us. (ibid.)

Christ has freed us through His atoning work. It is a glorious freedom. His freedom should lead us to rest in Him and to rejoice in Him. His freedom should cause us to do what He wants us to do, and that is not to submit to the yoke of slavery.

Christ Has Set Us Free: Live in the Truth
GALATIANS 5:2-12

The Galatians were not running in the truth. They were listening to the message of bondage. In verses 2-12 Paul confronts false teachers. He sustains his argument until verse 12, where he ends with a bang!

Again, a big problem is the belief in the necessity of circumcision and keeping the law. For Paul, circumcision symbolized the religion of human achievement instead of the religion of divine grace. Human achievement religion was slavery.

From this passage, we can pick out four results of the false teachers' message and five characteristics of false messengers. Here Paul tells us what happens if you buy into the Galatians' "Jesus + something else" message.

A False Message

First, if you accept this false message, then you view Christ as insufficient (v. 2).
Salvation by human achievement sees Christ as not doing enough. "This
was tantamount to saying that Moses must be allowed to finish what
Christ had begun" (Stott, *Message of Galatians*, 133). But Jesus' work is
perfect! You cannot add to it or improve on it! Calvin writes, "Whoever
wants half of Christ loses the whole" (148).

Second, if you accept this message, you must obey all of the law (v. 3).
This false message of circumcision carries a further all-encompassing
obligation: observing the law in its every precept, "since this is what
their circumcision commits them to, and [they] are seeking to 'be justified by the law'" (Stott, *Message of Galatians*, 133). There was a policy of
gradualism: you start with this and you would then do more observance
of the ceremonial law. Paul has already said in 3:10 that no one can
keep the law.

*Third, if you accept this message, then you are turning away from the doc-
trine of grace (v. 4).* Many have used this as a proof text that you can lose
your salvation, but that is not what Paul is saying. We know this based
on his other texts, and more precisely based on the context here. Paul
is talking about falling away from the *doctrine* of grace. If you believe
salvation is by the law, you have abandoned the belief that salvation is
by grace. He says that you cannot have it both ways: either salvation is
by divine accomplishment (Christ died for our sins) or it is by human
achievement (your good works).

Fourth, if you accept this message, you lose the hope of future glory (v. 5).
Paul says, "For through the Spirit, by faith, we eagerly wait for *the hope of
righteousness*" (emphasis added). Righteousness is ours now (2 Cor 5:21),
but we await our glorification with Christ (2 Tim 4:8). We are declared
righteous, but our righteousness is hidden from the world. It will be
unveiled on the last day. On that day, it will be undeniable.

How did we get this hope? We received that hope by trusting in
Christ by grace alone. The hymn writer said it best: "My hope is built on
nothing less, than Jesus' blood and righteousness" (Mote, "My Hope is
Built"). This hope keeps us running! Samuel Rutherford said, "If Christ
Jesus be the period, the end and lodging-home, at the end of your journey, there is no fear, ye go to a friend . . . ye may look death in the face
with joy" ("The Loveliness of Christ").

Until then, liberated people live "by faith" as they "eagerly wait for"
the hope of righteousness (v. 5). Further, Paul says, circumcision does

not matter, but "faith working through love" does (v. 6). Here we have the virtues or marks of a justified believer: faith, hope, and love. Works-based righteousness leads to fear, bondage, and despair; oh, the contrast of believing in the doctrine of grace and trusting in the finished work of Christ!

Paul says the false teacher's message is ultimately empty. He says circumcision does not accomplish anything (v. 6). Near the end of the letter, Paul says that what counts is "a new creation" (6:15). The teaching of the gospel is not empty. It is life changing. It leads to a life of "faith working through love." That is, love is the fruit of saving faith. (Paul expands on this concept more in 5:13-15 and 22.) False teachers were all about this external ritual; Paul says the Christian life is about faith that is demonstrated through loving service.

False Messengers

Notice the characteristics of the false messengers in Galatia. They seem to be typical of all false teachers.

First, false messengers hinder obedience to the truth (v. 7). This was true in Galatia, and false teachers certainly hinder people from obeying the truth today.

Second, false messengers are not from God. Paul says, "This persuasion did not come from the One who called you" (v. 8). We know God did not send them because they were teaching a false gospel of circumcision. Regardless of whether someone tells you that God "called" them or "sent" them, do not believe them if they are not teaching the true gospel. Paul says let them be eternally condemned, not embraced (Gal 1:7-9)!

Third, false messengers contaminate others. Paul says, "A little yeast leavens the whole lump of dough" (5:9). False teachers are like yeast that permeates all the bread dough and makes it rise. In the New Testament, yeast is often a symbol of permeating sin and false doctrine. Jesus said, "Beware of the yeast of the Pharisees and Sadducees" (Matt 16:6). False teachers are so problematic because they affect so many people. This is why Paul is so intense in this letter.

Fourth, false messengers will be judged (v. 10). He writes, "I have confidence in the Lord you will not accept any other view. But whoever it is that is confusing you will pay the penalty." As for those hearing the false teachers, Paul has confidence that those who were truly in Christ would not be persuaded by the false message. He believes at least some of the

Galatians will eventually detect the error and walk in the truth. As for the false teachers, he is confident that God will judge them.

Fifth, false messengers persecute true teachers (v. 11). Paul is being persecuted because he is preaching the gospel. You would think that to preach something that is freely available to all people would be accepted, but it is not. Why then? Paul was being persecuted for one simple reason: The cross offends people. People would rather you make much of them and preach a salvation-by-works system than to stand up and brag on Jesus and the cross and point people to Him as the only way.

I have a friend who recently shared about some attenders in his congregation. He said, "They told me they would not be back because they were deeply offended by the exclusive claims of the gospel." The cross: it is either a stumbling block, or it is the power of God for salvation (1 Cor 1:18). You either boast in it, or mock it and reject its power.

Why does the cross offend? It crushes human pride. It obliterates the religion of human achievement. For this crowd, it wiped out the idea that you were saved by keeping the Mosaic laws.

In one of Paul's most colorful statements, he says, "I wish those who are disturbing you might also get themselves castrated!" (v. 12). I have said some coarse things, but I have not used this line! It illustrates Paul's disgust and his passion. The gospel meant everything to Paul. If we really cared about the gospel and people's souls, we too would want false teachers to cease from existence.

This argument is summarized simply in this: Trust in Christ's atoning work alone for salvation. Find your righteousness in Him. Resist anyone who points you somewhere other than to Christ alone.

Christ Has Set Us Free: Live to Love and Serve
GALATIANS 5:13-15

There are two things Paul wants us to avoid about Christian freedom: *legalism* (trying to earn acceptance before God by works) and *license* (misapplying the doctrine of grace). In verses 13-15 Paul addresses the temptation to license. He talks about the moral law in a positive sense. Paul shows that freedom from the law does not do away with the obligations of holy conduct. Rather, justified people are now free to do what Christ wants! He says that part of being free from sin's slavery is that we are free to love and free to serve! This freedom represents the fulfillment of the Old Testament law of love. This subject of love continues in

Galatians 5:22 and 6:1-4. Here we see the call to love one another and our neighbors.

Negatively, Paul says, "Don't use this freedom as an opportunity for the flesh" (v. 13). The "flesh" does not refer to that which clothes our bony skeletons, but our fallen human nature. We are prone to drift spiritually because of our flesh. Christian freedom is not a freedom *to sin* but a freedom *from sin*. Christian freedom is a freedom to enjoy serving others and pursuing godliness. Do not live to gratify the desires of the flesh. That is an abuse of freedom and a misunderstanding of freedom.

Positively, Paul says that because we are free let us "serve one another through love" (v. 13), fulfilling the law of "Love your neighbor as yourself" (v. 14). "Serve" is actually the word for "slave" (Stott, *Message of Galatians*, 141–42). Paul has said, "Don't be a slave," but now he says, "You are free to be a slave." Luther put it well: "A Christian is free and independent in every respect, a bond servant to none. A Christian is a dutiful servant in every respect, owing a duty to everyone" (George, 378). It is a paradox. The Galatians were free from bondage and under grace. But Paul says that they were now free to love and serve others. It is as if he says, "If you want a law, here is one: love" (cf. 6:2). But the difference in Paul's exhortation is that it is fueled by the Spirit (5:16–6:10), and it is not done in an effort to earn righteousness. When it comes to loving our neighbors as ourselves, we must remember that keeping the entire law for our justification is unattainable, but Jesus fulfilled it for us. Now, as a result of our faith in Him, by the power of the Holy Spirit, we are free to live out the moral teaching of the law. The Spirit changes us and empowers us to obey God.

It is surprising that Paul does not say, "Love God and neighbor," as Jesus taught. Perhaps this is shorthand, or maybe he has the Galatian setting in mind and just wants to mention love because of the context. But more likely, he has in mind the idea that love for God manifests itself in love for neighbors. The two are inseparable.

The call to freedom, then, is a call to oneness in Christ and to loving service within the believing community. The Galatians were not saved to be a group of isolated individuals. And neither were we. We are brought out of bondage to live in community. A lot of Christians follow the American way of life more than the Bible. Americans love individuality and autonomy and anonymity in church. But Christianity is about living in community (cf. 6:1-10). Look at this verse! Christ saved you, liberated you so that you could be so committed to others that it looks like slavery! Do not presume you are growing when you are not in community. Do not be a Christian ninja, just sliding in and out of worship services without anyone seeing you! The Lord saved us so we could love and serve others.

The call to freedom also means that we are free from using people. We are free from seeking approval from people. We are free from self-promotion. Instead, we are to live out of the overflow of a heart that has been set free by Christ and to serve others lovingly.

Paul adds that love does not look like biting and devouring one another or being "consumed by one another" (5:15). These words refer to animal-like behavior. If we go around taking chunks out of one another, then we will consume one another like ravenous sharks or hyenas. Paul is probably speaking of malicious talk and gossip. Such practice is the opposite of the outworking of the fruit of the Spirit that leads to kindness, gentleness, and goodness.

In sum, Paul says that Christ has set us free! So let us live free, resting and rejoicing in Christ. Let us live in the truth, not believing the message of false teachers. Let us love and serve others.

In the movie *Chariots of Fire* (1981), Eric Liddell speaks that famous line, "When I run, I feel His pleasure." While you may not like physical running, I pray that you will feel the pleasure of God as you run in the freedom of the gospel. Feel the pleasure of not being guilty, of overcoming the grip of sin, of not being enslaved to legalism; feel the pleasure of living by the Spirit; feel the pleasure of having access to God, being accepted by God; feel the pleasure of having a secure future with God; and feel the pleasure of loving and serving one another and your neighbors as yourself.

You are free to run. Do not let anyone hinder you.

Reflect and Discuss

1. Respond to this sentiment: Adding a little to the gospel is not a major problem, as long as we believe in the cross.
2. What does it mean to be set free by Christ?
3. Does eternal security give us freedom to sin without fear of the consequences? Explain. How do many in our culture define freedom? How does Paul define it?
4. What's the difference between the kind of work that misses God's grace and the kind that pleases Him?

5. Does the phrase "fallen from grace" (5:4) refer to losing your salvation? If not, then what does it mean?
6. If we are already made righteous in Christ, then to what does the phrase "the hope of righteousness" (5:5) refer?
7. Explain the difference between hope as the Bible defines it and hope as many people use the word today.
8. What was your reaction to Paul's words in 5:12? Why do you think he said that?
9. Why should our freedom in Christ lead us to a life of love for one another and our neighbors?
10. Have you ever seen people in the church "bite and devour one another?" (5:15). What were the causes? How does this passage speak to this problem?

Walk by the Spirit

GALATIANS 5:16-26

Main Idea: By the power of the Holy Spirit, believers may conquer the desires of the flesh, which constantly threaten them.

I. **Walk by the Spirit (5:16-18).**
    A. We must continually walk by the Spirit (5:16a).
    B. We must walk by the Spirit to conquer the flesh (5:16b).
    C. We must walk by the Spirit because the battle is intense (5:17).
    D. We must walk by the Spirit to be free from the law (5:18).
II. **Observe the Obvious (5:19-23).**
    A. The works of the flesh (5:19-21)
    B. The fruit of the Spirit (5:22-23)
III. **Remember the Good News (5:24-26).**
    A. Believers belong to Christ Jesus (5:24).
    B. Believers possess the Spirit (5:25-26).

In the previous passage we looked at how Paul called the Galatians to freedom. They were called to manifest their freedom in Christ through loving service to others (vv. 13-15). In Galatians 5:16-25 Paul builds on this idea to explain how such freedom and progress can only come through the power of the Spirit. The Galatians were drifting into a works-based, flesh-driven faith, but Paul calls them to a life of liberty in Christ and Spirit-filled fruitfulness.

The passage basically divides into three main parts. First, in verses 16-18 Paul describes the need to walk by the Spirit. Second, in verses 19-23 he highlights the evidences of a life lived in the flesh versus a life lived in the Spirit. Third, in verse 24 Paul says that those who truly "belong to Christ" have put to death the desires of the flesh, giving them power to deal with the remaining effects of the flesh. A question is, What should we do with verses 25-26? Do these verses belong in this passage or in the following passage, which speaks of responsibilities within the household of faith (see Schreiner's discussion, *Galatians*, 353)? Regardless of the placement, one can see how Galatians 5 and 6 are closely tied together. A Spirit-led life will lead to fruitfulness and will manifest itself in practical acts of love and service, not in the fleshly acts of being "conceited, provoking one another, envying one another" (v. 26). I have chosen to place these final two verses with verse 24, but my exposition of 6:1-10 will allude to 5:25-26 as well.

This passage is very important in light of a Christian's desire to spiritually grow. How do we bear the fruit of the Spirit mentioned in this text? How can we grow as God's adopted children? Let us take these three main divisions and make three points of application: (1) walk by the Spirit, (2) observe the obvious, and (3) remember the good news.

Walk by the Spirit
GALATIANS 5:16-18

Clearly the focus of this passage is on the need to live constantly by the power of the Spirit (vv. 16,18,25). Paul is not talking to "super Christians" in this passage. He does not tell only the leaders or the "charismatic types" to live by the Spirit. Are you a parent? Then you need this passage! Are you single? Then you need this passage! Are you a teenager? Then you need this passage! Every believer needs to learn how to walk by the Spirit, so Paul tells all believers to do so. Paul is still aggressive in this new unit, as proven by the "I say" comment. It appears he is still addressing false teachers as he attempts to explain the nature of the Christian life in greater detail. He tells us four important truths about walking by the Spirit.

We Must Continually Walk by the Spirit (5:16a)

To "walk" by the Spirit indicates the need to yield to the Spirit every day: at work, at a ball game, in the home, everywhere. The word for walk, *peripateite*, in its wider usage in Greek means "to walk around after someone or to walk in a particular direction" (George, *Galatians*, 386). In the days of Aristotle, his students were known as *peripatetics* because of their habit of following their teacher around (ibid.). For the Christian, to walk by the Spirit, or to be led by the Sprit, means to follow our Teacher around. We must listen to the Spirit's Word, discern His will, and follow His guidance. This is not a deeper life or higher life; this is the normal Christian life.

We should note the tension here between God's divine power and the believer's human choice (Schreiner, *Galatians*, 343). Christians must decide to walk by the Spirit continually, and at the same time the Spirit is at work to create new appetites and give new power to resist the flesh and to please God.

We Must Walk by the Spirit to Conquer the Flesh (5:16b)

The phrase "and you will not carry out the desire of the flesh" is a promise. Those who yield to the Spirit daily have the promise that they will not gratify their fallen human nature. We should see that there is no neutral ground here. We are living in one sphere or the other. Either we are submitting to the Spirit's leadership, or we are gratifying our flesh. If we are submitting to the Spirit, we cannot gratify the flesh. You cannot pray and look at pornography at the same time. The way you deal with your sin is not simply by saying "no" to the flesh, but by also saying "yes" to the Spirit's work.

Conquering the flesh does not merely come from theological knowledge. A professor of theology can be addicted to pornography or fly off the handle in rage just the same as a younger believer with little theological knowledge. Growth does not happen because of your ability. Sadly, I have known several gifted ministers who are no longer in ministry because they were not walking by the Spirit. They gave in to various temptations of the flesh and suffered tragic consequences, wrecking themselves and others. Growth does not happen because you attend seminars or read books, as helpful as they may be. God changes us from the inside out through the Spirit. We must daily yield to Him so that we do not gratify the desires of the flesh.

We Must Walk by the Spirit Because the Battle Is Intense (5:17)

Paul alluded to the "present evil age" in 1:4. Building on this, he says that the flesh is against the Spirit and vice versa, and that these two are "opposed" to each other. In verse 16 Paul explains this battle; in verse 17 he stresses the intensity of it. Part of the problem with fighting the flesh is a casual attitude toward sin that the enemy wants us to have. Paul is telling us that the Christian life is a war. Therefore, to conquer the flesh, one must see the seriousness of this battle and resolve to walk by the Spirit.

Do you recognize what kind of war you are in? You face the world's temptations, Satan's temptations, and the flesh's temptations. Do not allow yourself to take a complacent posture in the Christian life. Do not imagine that you are somehow absolved from this fight, or assume that the flesh will not entice you.

In Romans 7:14-25 Paul illustrates the intensity of the battle. The mighty apostle did not treat this battle lightly. We will fight with the flesh until the coming of Christ. It is an intense, ongoing war.

Some imagine that if you could just live apart from the culture's temptations, then you would not have to deal with sin. Yeah, right! The problem is not simply "out there" (in the world); the problem is "in here" (in the flesh). G. K. Chesterton once responded to a newspaper article that invited people to respond to the question, "What's wrong with the world?" His reply was simple: "I am" (Harvey, *When Sinners Say I Do*, 52).

The church father Jerome described how removing oneself from the culture does not remove temptation from one's heart:

> Oh, how often I imagined that I was in the midst of the pleasures of Rome when I was stationed in the desert, in that solitary wasteland which is so burned up by the heat of the sun that it provides a dreadful habitation for the monks! I, who because of the fear of hell had condemned myself to such a hell and who had nothing but scorpions and wild animals for company, often thought I was dancing with a chorus of girls. My face was pale from fasting, but my mind burned with passionate desires within my freezing body, and the fires of sex seethed. (George, *Galatians*, 388)

Did you catch that? He was in a desert, but the desires of the flesh still seethed. We cannot escape this battle completely until Christ finally delivers us.

This principle of dealing with our own hearts needs to be learned by everyone; doing so would definitely improve marriages. In *When Sinners Say I Do*, Dave Harvey writes, "What if you abandoned the idea that the problems and weakness in your marriage are caused by lack of information, dedication, or communication? What if you saw your problems as they truly are: caused by a war within your heart?" (Harvey, *Sinners*, 29). If a husband or wife walks in the flesh, not the Spirit, then there will be devastating results. Both people must deal with their own hearts if they want to live in harmony. The same is true for other relationships also (cf. Jas 4:1-2).

Why is this battle so intense? Paul says it is because the flesh and the Spirit have competing agendas. The flesh wants to make it so "you don't do what you want" (Gal 5:17). Though we want to do good as believers, there are times when we cry out with Paul, "What a wretched man I am! Who will rescue me from this dying body? I thank God through Jesus Christ our Lord!" (Rom 7:24-25). The new day has dawned for Christians. They are new creations, but the battle rages on until Christ returns. Still, the believer can have "substantial, significant, and observable victory over the flesh" (Schreiner, 345).

John Newton describes his own personal battle with life as described in Galatians 5:17. He wrote, "I [do not want] to be the sport of prey of wild, fain, foolish, and worse imaginations; but this evil is present with me: my heart is like a highway, like a city without walls or gates" (Harvey, *Sinners*, 49). Can you identify with him? We must walk by the Spirit because the battle is intense.

We Must Walk by the Spirit to Be Free from the Law (18)

What does Paul mean by saying, "But if you are led by the Spirit, *you are not under the law*" (emphasis added)? It is probably best to translate "if" as "since" (Schreiner, *Galatians*, 345). Those who are "led" by the Spirit (cf. Rom 8:14; Luke 4:1; Isa 63:11-15) are not "under the law," meaning that they no longer belong to the old era of redemptive history (ibid.). Paul already described in this letter that living under the law leads to being "under a curse" (3:10), "under sin's power" (3:22), "under a guardian" (3:25), "in slavery under the elemental forces of the world" (4:3), and in need of redemption (4:5) (ibid.).

Therefore, the point is that life in the Spirit brings a whole new way of life. This verse does not mean that you have freedom to sin, but a freedom from sin. You have new desires and new power to please God by bearing the fruit of the Spirit. Do not live under the crushing weight of the law, but live by the dynamic power of the Spirit.

Observe the Obvious
GALATIANS 5:19-23

How does one know if he or she is walking by the Spirit? Paul tells us in verses 19-23. It is not difficult to tell! Paul lists the virtues of the Spirit and the vices of the flesh. Schreiner says, "those things that issue from the flesh are obvious and clear to anyone with an ounce of discernment" (Schreiner, *Galatians*, 346).

The Works of the Flesh (19-20)

Paul first catalogues a nasty list of sinful desires and actions that can helpfully be organized into four areas: sex, religion, relationships, and indulgences. With this categorization, we should note that there is some overlap (as with sexual immorality and relational sins). Further, we should realize that this list is not exhaustive. The phrase "and anything similar" makes it clear that these are simply examples.

Catalogues of vices were popular in Paul's day, and we find other examples in Scripture, like in Romans 1:29-31 and 2 Timothy 3:2-5. No two lists are the same in literature or the Bible. All of the works of the flesh arise from a problem with our hearts, as Jesus made clear (Mark 7:20-23). So I do not think it is imperative to go through each sin in great detail, since these are simply examples of the works of the flesh. They are worth considering to be sure, but they are not an exhaustive list.

Sex (v. 19). Interestingly, Paul notes sexual sin first in his other lists (cf. Eph 5:3; 1 Cor 6:9; Col 3:5). So does Jesus in Mark 7:21-22. Here Paul uses the terms "sexual immorality" *(porneia),* "moral impurity," and "promiscuity." The first term is a general word for all forms of sexual sin. Moral impurity often denotes sexual sin also (cf. Rom 1:24; 2 Cor 12:21; 1 Thess 4:7). Promiscuity is also a common word for sexual sin (cf. Mark 7:22; Rom 13:13; 1 Pet 4:3; 2 Pet 2:2,7,18). It emphasizes lack of restraint and unbridled passions.

Sexual sin is a major problem for many reasons. Sexual sin with another person (either physically or through other forms of *porneia*) grieves the Holy Spirit. It affects many others, not just the one sinning. It displays a graphic self-centeredness. It dishonors those made in the image of God. It violates God's pure plan for marriage. It is totally opposite of the fruit of the Spirit, especially *love.*

Religion (v. 20). While James speaks of such a thing as "pure and undefiled religion" (Jas 1:27), I am using the term *religion* negatively here. Simply being religious does not imply walking by the Spirit. Various religious expressions exist all over the world. It may look like "idolatry" or it may look like "sorcery," but it is fruitless religion.

The mention of idolatry demonstrates how everyone worships someone or something. The question is, Who or what are people worshiping? Those engaged in idolatry are refusing to worship the true and living God alone. They are living out Romans 1:21-25, worshiping created things instead of Creator God.

Sorcery involves the practice of trying to manipulate circumstances or dark powers to bring about a desired goal rather than submitting to and trusting in God alone. Today people read horoscopes to find meaning, and many believe superstitious actions will somehow manipulate events. This is the work of the flesh.

Idolatry is not merely a vile practice of those in other religions. Idolatry is a heart issue. People commit idolatry when they look to something other than God to give them what only God can give them. These desires include salvation, peace, security, joy, and provision. Money, mentioned throughout the Bible, is a big idol today (e.g., Matt 6:24; Col 3:5). American money may say, "In God we trust," but in reality many trust in the bills themselves, which is why when the economy tanked, people lost their minds and took their lives.

Relationships (vv. 20-21). Paul notes eight works of the flesh associated with relational sins, which highlights the focus on relationships in Galatians 5:13–6:10. Some of these sins overlap. Allow me to explicate Paul's list:

- *Hatreds* refers to enmity of any kind. It is at the root of conflict.
- *Strife* means to have contentious temper. Paul uses this term in other lists (cf. Rom 1:29; 13:13; 2 Cor 12:20; 1 Tim 6:4; 1 Cor 1:11; 3:3; Phil 1:5; Titus 3:9).
- *Jealousy* sometimes has a positive meaning, but here it is clearly negative. A jealous person wants what someone else possesses. This sin often leads to other sins like bitterness and violence. Those who are jealous demonstrate a lack of gratitude to God for His providence and a lack of love for others.
- *Outbursts of anger* appears elsewhere in Paul's lists of vices (cf. 2 Cor 12:20; Eph 4:31). It refers to the eruption of the person with an uncontrolled temper. We should not try to excuse this sin by making it a personality trait or a cultural trait. Paul says it is a work of the flesh.
- *Selfish ambitions* was a term derived from the political arena in Greece to denote "office seeking" (George, *Galatians*, 395). It appears elsewhere in Paul's writings. One of those occasions includes Paul's description of some preachers who preached with impure motives. They preached "out of rivalry, not sincerely" (Phil 1:17; cf. Rom 2:8; 2 Cor 12:20; Jas 3:14,16). Such attitudes are evidences of living by the flesh, not the Spirit.

- *Dissentions* appears in one other place: Romans 16:17. Paul told the Romans to stay away from people who cause dissention or division. Paul's warning not to "bite and devour one another" reflects this sin (Gal 5:15). The Spirit brings unity, but the flesh brings division.
- *Factions* is closely related to the previous term and in some instances stands for false teaching (Schreiner, *Galatians*, 347). Here it emphasizes the "party spirit" that creates division where there should be no division (cf. 1 Cor 11:19).
- *Envy* is also present in other lists (cf. Rom 1:29; 1 Tim 6:4; Titus 3:3) and is similar to *jealousy*. The envious person is not happy with God's gifts and cannot stand it when others succeed.

Indulgence (v. 21). In this final group of sins, Paul mentions "drunkenness" and "carousing." Those who cannot control their appetites obviously demonstrate a life dominated by the flesh, not the Spirit. These two sins are mentioned together elsewhere (cf. 1 Pet 4:3; Rom 13:13).

The Warning (v. 21). Paul has led us down into the pit of depravity by highlighting these works of the flesh. He has shown us the ugliness of the flesh. Then he ends with a warning: "those who practice such things will not inherit the kingdom of God." In other words, if you are living under the rule of the flesh, then you should stand in fear because you will not enter the coming kingdom. Those who come to faith in Christ by grace alone are new people (6:15). While they will still wrestle with sin, the flesh will not dominate them. They have new desires and new power to live. Our good works do not save us, but true salvation leads to fruitfulness and faithfulness.

The Fruit of the Spirit (5:22-23)

The list of vices is contrasted with a list of nine virtues, as noted by the conjunction "But." Schreiner notes that the list has no discernable order apart from "love" appearing first. Others group the list into three parts. Stott says that they portray the Christian's attitude toward God, to other people, and to oneself (*Message of Galatians*, 148). George says that they are grouped into three triads (love, joy, and peace/patience, kindness, and goodness/faith, gentleness, and self-control) to give a sense of order, although there is no attempt to provide an exhaustive list of virtues (*Galatians*, 398). The categorizations are helpful for memory and for personal reflection, so I have chosen to use them, even though

I would not argue that such a classification is intended. I agree with George that this list is probably not exhaustive, since other virtues are mentioned elsewhere (like hope and godliness).

I do think it is significant that love appears first based upon the surrounding context of Galatians. There is a clear focus on love in the passage before and after (5:13-15; 6:1-2). Paul is showing where the power for love comes from: the Spirit. Further, some of the other virtues mentioned in this list are practical expressions of love itself (patience, kindness, faithfulness, gentleness; cf. 1 Cor 13). While Paul addresses more than love, this particular virtue is clearly highlighted.

Paul says "fruit" not "fruits." This probably points to the fact that all of these collectively make up Christlikeness. As we abide in Christ, all of "the fruits" of the Spirit get produced. That is not to say that each one is as strong in us as the others, but simply that the Spirit is shaping us in every way into Christlikeness. Additionally, the fruit of the Spirit as a whole is basically a character sketch of Christ. What is the Spirit doing in us? He is conforming us into the image of Jesus, the One who perfectly embodied love and every other virtue mentioned.

Before looking at them in three triads, remember that our goal in looking at this list is not to observe the virtues and then try to make ourselves better in our own strength. The tendency is to look at each one and say, "I'm doing all right here, but not here," or, "OK, I need to work on patience now." Rather, the point is that you must walk by the Spirit, and then the virtues grow out of that relationship with God. As a parent, I would also love to "staple on fruit" to my kids. But these virtues must flow from our union with Christ, not from our own behavior modification. We might get our kids' behavior or our own to improve, but we will not be able to create Christlikeness apart from the Spirit's work. We all need new hearts. Regenerate people have the power to naturally, holistically, and gradually bear fruit.

Love, Joy, Peace. It should not surprise us that "love" is mentioned first, given the emphasis on it elsewhere. John says that love is evidence that we know God (1 John 4:7-8). Paul talks about the primacy of love in between two chapters on the work of the Spirit (1 Cor 13). Paul tells the Romans that the Spirit has poured His love into us (Rom 5:5). Spirit-led believers express a sincere love for others (1 John 3:11-18) and express their love for God, who "first loved us" (1 John 4:19). Schreiner says, "Love is the heart and soul of the Pauline ethic, for it is love that fulfills the law (Rom 13:8-10; Gal 5:14)" (Schreiner, *Galatians,* 349).

The Spirit also produces "joy" (cf. Rom 14:17). Believers can have joy even in the midst of trials because the Spirit has given us new affections (cf. 2 Cor 6:10). We are called on to "rejoice always" (1 Thess 5:16). This peculiar joy in Christians is vividly illustrated in the life of the early church in the books of Acts, where the work of the Spirit and joy are related. For example, Luke writes about Paul and Barnabas being driven out of the Galatian region: "And the disciples were filled with joy and the Holy Spirit" (Acts 13:52). The Spirit produces a life of satisfying joy, while living in the flesh only leads to constant dissatisfaction.

The Spirit also creates "peace" in the life of a Spirit-led believer. Believers have the peace of God made possible through the cross work of Jesus (Eph 2:14-15,17). Peace rules the hearts of those who walk by the Spirit (cf. Col 3:15). Spirit-led Christians will also take on the role of peacemakers by the Spirit's power (cf. Eph 4:1-6).

Patience, Kindness, Goodness. Paul mentions "patience" in other lists (2 Cor 6:6; Eph 4:2; Col 3:12; 2 Tim 3:10). Enduring situations and putting up with difficult people is not easy. We need the Spirit's power to deal with our own children, people in traffic, and those "interruptions" during the day. I even found myself growing impatient with my kids as I wrote on the fruit of the Spirit! How we need to remember how patient God is with us and to pray for the Spirit to work in us!

Believers imitate Christ through "kindness" also. By His grace and kindness, God brought us repentance and faith in Christ (Rom 2:4; Eph 2:7; Titus 3:4). We should thus be marked by lives of kindness expressed through acts of service, generosity, and hospitality.

"Goodness" is closely related to kindness (cf. Rom 15:14; Eph 5:9; 2 Thess 1:11). It speaks to the idea of doing good deeds and being generous. Paul later says that believers should "do good to everyone, and especially to those who are of the household of faith" (Gal 6:10 ESV).

Faith, Gentleness, Self-control. The person known for "faith" or "faithfulness" is the reliable and dependable person. He keeps his word and fulfills his promises. Paul told Timothy to look for "faithful men" and entrust them with teaching others the gospel (2 Tim 2:2). One of the most difficult things to do in the Christian faith is to be faithful to your assignment in hard times. It takes the work of the Spirit to produce such steadfastness in life, ministry, and marriage.

Paul mentions "gentleness" in other lists as well (Eph 4:2; Col 3:12; Titus 3:2). In the next chapter, Paul highlights the need to restore the wayward brother "with a gentle spirit" (Gal 6:1). He urges Timothy to deal with his opponents gently in order that they may repent (2 Tim 2:25). Jesus, the gentle Savior, invites the weary to come and rest in Him (Matt 11:29). Pastors are to imitate Jesus in displaying a life of gentleness and meekness, not violence (1 Tim 3:3).

Finally, Paul ends this amazing list of Christlike qualities with "self-control." In contrast to the works of the flesh, like drunkenness and orgies, those who walk by the Spirit live restrained lives. The Spirit enables believers to have mastery over their passions. George says, "The fact that self-control appears last in Paul's list may indicate its importance as a summation of the preceding virtues" (*Galatians*, 404). In our flesh we are out of control, but by the Spirit we live self-controlled lives.

How can one live a life filled with such traits as these nine qualities? Paul says, by the Spirit. It does not happen by the law, for he says, "Against such things there is no law" (v. 23). In other words, you cannot legislate these qualities. The law can never produce this kind of fruitfulness.

Paul tells us to walk by the Spirit, and then he gives us marks of the flesh and of the Spirit and tells us to observe the obvious. So pause and ask some questions. Is the fruit of the Spirit evident in your life? Is the character of Christ being formed in you? Perhaps you can say, "Yes, but I would love more progress." Join the crowd. The Spirit grows us gradually and painfully. But He produces fruit over time, as we yield to the Spirit and put to death the flesh. This leads us to the third major point.

Remember the Good News
GALATIANS 5:24-26

One could read this passage and be led to the conclusion that the Christian life is a tug-of-war, and "believers are consigned to a spiritually meager existence of perpetual defeat and minimal growth" (George, *Galatians*, 404). But I want to point out the good news mentioned here! Paul tells the Galatian believers that they should recognize the hope and power they have in their new identity. They are not hopeless in this battle, and they are not powerless. Two matters should encourage us here.

Believers Belong to Christ Jesus (5:24)

We do not need the law to restrain our behavior, since we "have crucified the flesh with its passions and desires" (v. 24). Something more radical and powerful has happened to us. We have crucified the flesh. When did that happen? Paul seems to be referring to our conversion, since "Those who are in Adam and in the flesh do not have the resources to crucify it" (Schreiner, *Galatians*, 351). The verb "crucified" points us back to Galatians 2:20 (ibid.). When people intentionally, purposefully trust in Christ alone for salvation (the past-tense, active verb here in 5:24, "*have* crucified"), they are uniting themselves with Christ and saying no to their life in Adam. This death to the flesh brings about a new creation and a deliverance from the present evil age (1:4).

While believers still feel the temptation to sin, fleshly passions no longer have to reign. The good news is that because you belong to Jesus, you do not have to be dominated by the flesh. You and the flesh have parted ways. Something has already happened decisively at the cross. Christ has won the ultimate battle, and now we have to deal with this mop-up operation until Christ comes to deliver us completely from this body of death (Rom 7:24-25).

While we must daily "mortify the flesh" by acts of fasting, self-control, prayer, and repentance (George, *Galatians*, 405), our ultimate hope is that we belong to Jesus. So the question is, Do you? Are you Christ's? Have you become a new creation? If so, then you have power to slay the desires of the flesh, though it will be a daily and sometimes painful battle.

Believers Possess the Spirit (5:25-26)

Not only has our identity changed at conversion, but we also now have power to live every day by the Spirit. Paul says, "Since we live by the Spirit, we must also follow the Spirit." Again, while the passage reminds us of the intensity of the battle, we should be encouraged. We belong to Jesus, and we have the Holy Spirit. When we know these facts, it gives us enormous hope to face our daily battles. Stott says, "This victory is within the reach of every Christian, for every Christian has 'crucified the flesh' (v. 24) and every Christian 'lives by the Spirit'" (*Message of Galatians*, 154). We have what we need for victory.

What must we do then? In verse 24 we noted that the privileged position we have (belonging to Jesus) does not mean we have nothing to do. We must strive to daily kill the flesh, but because we are Christ's, we do not have to fear that we will be dominated by it. Here in verse 25 our possession of the Spirit does not leave us without a responsibility. Paul says, "we must also follow the Spirit" or "keep in step with the

Spirit" (ESV). George says this verb had a military meaning, referring to "stand in a row" or to "be drawn up in line" (*Galatians*, 406). For the believer, we are to walk in the Spirit under the leadership of the Spirit. What a privilege to have the Spirit leading us! Keep in step with the Spirit in your attitude, conduct, relationships, and ministry.

In verse 26 Paul gives one exhortation that draws our attention back to 5:15. He says, "We must not become conceited, provoking one another, envying one another" (v. 26). The fruit of the Spirit is love, not conceit and envy. Paul bookends his instruction on how not to relate to one another in the church (5:15,26) around this section of the war between the flesh and the Spirit, once again showing us that the Christian life is a Spirit-led life. To love and serve one another in the household of faith rightly, we must remember that we belong to Jesus and that we possess the Holy Spirit. We must then resolve to live daily by the Spirit so that we do not gratify the desires of the flesh. In the following chapter, Paul will give more examples about how to positively care for others by the Spirit.

Reflect and Discuss

1. Describe the conflict believers have with the flesh.
2. Compare and contrast this passage with Romans 7:13-25.
3. What struck you the most in the section on "The Works of the Flesh"?
4. What lesson or reminder did you need the most in the section on "The Fruit of the Spirit"?
5. What is the "good news" in this passage?
6. How might you daily crucify the flesh?
7. What means or method does this passage teach for becoming like Christ? In what aspects do we not become like Christ?
8. How does this passage relate to the passages before and after it (5:13-16 and 6:1-10)?
9. In what ways are you tempted to disobey verse 26? Stop and pray for the Spirit's work in you to avoid this sin. List ways you might instead love and serve others.
10. How might the application of this passage change a couple's marriage?

Responsibilities of Spirit-Led Believers

GALATIANS 6:1-10

Main Idea: Paul urges Spirit-led believers to recognize and execute the practical responsibilities of the household of faith.

I. **Gentle Restoration (6:1)**
   A. The context of restoration: family
   B. The need for restoration
   C. The nature of restoration
   D. The nature of the restorer
II. **Humble Burden Bearing (6:2-5)**
   A. Burdens are a reality in a fallen world (6:2a).
   B. We are not self-sufficient (6:2a).
   C. Burden bearing is a command to all believers (6:2a).
   D. Burden bearing is how we fulfill the law of Christ (6:2b).
   E. Pride hinders burden bearing (6:3-4).
   F. Paul distinguishes between heavy burdens and light loads (6:5).
III. **Generous Sharing (6:6)**
   A. Responsibilities of the teacher
   B. Responsibilities of the receiver
IV. **Personal Holiness (6:7-8)**
V. **Practical Goodness (6:9-10)**

In the last chapter, we looked at life in the Spirit. Paul described the nature of a Spirit-controlled life. So, what does it look like practically to "walk by the Spirit" (5:16), to be "led by the Spirit" (5:18), and to "live by the Spirit" (5:25)? What are the results of Spirit-filled living? People respond in different ways. The devotional types might say that it leads to better quiet times. The mystical types might say it leads to charismatic experiences. Miracle seekers might claim it leads to power encounters or signs and wonders.

While the Spirit certainly works in various ways to glorify Christ, allow me to put forward another idea that is too often overlooked in a discussion about what it looks like to live by the Spirit. Here is my big idea: chapter 6 comes after chapter 5! I know it is a crazy idea. But

I do have a PhD. Not everyone could figure this out! What I mean is that the lifestyle put forward in chapter 6 follows a great section on the Spirit in chapter 5. It is a continuation of the discussion on the Spirit. So what is chapter 6 about? It is about how life in the Spirit should lead Christians to live out their faith in *biblical community*. This passage speaks of the responsibilities that Spirit-filled believers, "you who are spiritual" (6:1), should have toward one another in the body of Christ. In fact, some connect 5:25-26 with these responsibilities to highlight the relationship between the Spirit and the proper attitudes Christians should have toward their brothers and sisters in Christ.

Paul follows the all-important passage about life in the Spirit with a very practical section. He says nothing about signs and wonders, and he does not go into detail about spiritual gifts. He talks about how the community of faith operates when the Spirit is leading. This is often overlooked: life in the Spirit involves healthy relationships within the body of Christ. It does not involve conceit and envy (5:26), but a life of love (5:22).

I remember hearing a story about a pastor in New York. A woman in the congregation said to him, "Pastor, we need to see more signs and wonders. We just haven't seen enough signs and wonders." The pastor responded, "Ma'am, over there sits a lady who has been evicted from her apartment with her children. I would consider it a sign and wonder if you would take them into your house to live for three months."

Perhaps you are like the first woman. You have a great desire for the miraculous. There is nothing wrong with wanting to see God do extraordinary things. But do not overlook and undervalue how the Spirit usually works in our lives: through the practical deeds of love for others, especially deeds performed within "the household of faith" (6:10).

Does it surprise you that many Christians talk about the Spirit's work in their lives but do not even belong to a local church? If a person simply goes from event to event, or only watches sermons at home, and does not have biblical community, then he or she is not applying the New Testament. God saves us and empowers us by the Spirit in order that we may live in community with believers who fulfill His mission in the world.

This is Christianity: loving one another. We live in this "Harry Potter" culture where people are isolated. Some are busy. But you can be busy and lonely. This is what researchers call "crowded loneliness." You need to replace crowded loneliness with biblical community.

Friday night I was at a leadership party. I asked the group, "What has been the biggest blessing since we started Imago Dei Church?" Not one person said, "the preaching." Virtually everyone noted the relationships. I take that as a sign of God's mighty work.

The first fruit of the Spirit mentioned is "love" (5:22; cf. 1 Cor 13). The Spirit works in us to help us love one another, not to devour one another (5:15) nor to provoke and envy one another (5:26). Instead of making this merely theoretical, Paul grounds this idea by showing some ways to love practically. Let us consider five practices of Spirit-led believers.

Gentle Restoration
GALATIANS 6:1

The Context of Restoration: Family

Paul says, "*Brothers*, if someone is caught in any wrongdoing, you who are spiritual should restore such a person with a gentle spirit, watching out for yourselves so you also won't be tempted" (6:1, emphasis added). Notice the familial language used. Paul begins by saying, "Brothers." The church is a family. You need a family to care for you spiritually. The church is a "household" (6:10) of brothers and sisters (cf. 6:18) who call God "*Abba*, Father!" (4:6). An outsider might think, "You've got a weird looking family!" Yes, it should be diverse. God likes variety.

There is nothing like the family of faith. Paul says to Timothy that the church should treat each other as brothers and sisters, mothers and fathers (1 Tim 5:1-2; cf. Mark 3:35). Do you love your church family? If so, care for them spiritually. I love my kids, and I don't want to see them destroy their lives. I want to protect them. At times, I have to correct them. But that is what families do. They care for each other by speaking truth in love.

One of the things God does through the gospel is form a people (cf. Titus 2:14). To be part of the family of God is a gift of the grace of God. Recognize the glory of it, and invest your life in it.

The Need for Restoration

Paul says that sometimes those in the family get "caught in . . . wrongdoing." They are clearly guilty of transgression. The enemy sets traps, and sometimes brothers and sisters fall into these traps. We need our faith family to pry open the traps and set us free when this happens. James refers to the idea of wandering from the truth:

> *My brothers, if anyone among you* wanders from the truth *and someone brings him back, let him know that whoever brings back a sinner* from his wandering *will save his soul from death and will cover a multitude of sins.* (Jas 5:19-20 ESV, emphasis added)

Are you concerned with straying church members? I lost Titus, our miniature schnauzer, one time. When I eventually found him, he was down the street in a neighbor's backyard, where my neighbor and friends were working out. But before we found him, you would have thought the world was coming to an end. Are you more concerned with your wandering pet than wandering Church members? I do not mean to belittle pets (I love them), but it seems that some in the church have no concern over the fact that a brother or sister is wandering away from the truth. Others take a "Well, it's not my business" approach when a brother is straying. It *is* your business when you realize that you are united to them by faith. The body suffers when a member is broken.

The church is not just a charitable organization like the Red Cross, the civic club, the Rotary, or Kiwanis. Those groups do some great work. But by its nature, the church is something different. We are brothers and sisters, adopted into God's family, knit together by the Holy Spirit in a common fellowship. We must seek the spiritual welfare of one another.

The Nature of Restoration

So what must we do? Paul says, "restore such a person" (6:1). Stott notes that this word *restore* means to put back in order, or to repair. It was the same word used for setting a fractured bone (*Message of Galatians*, 160). We are to put the broken one back together, like a doctor would do. It was the same word also used for mending fishnets (Mark 1:19). In the same way, the goal is to put the broken ones back together and release them for service. When Jesus gave the steps for church discipline in Matthew 18:15-17, the goal of the process was positive and constructive, as it is here (ibid.).

We should qualify this ministry, though. Do not take this as a command to be the "righteousness police," inspecting every detail of a person's life. I do not think that is what Paul has in mind. The matters highlighted here seem to be sins that are destroying people. These are not mere conscience issues.

For example, if a brother or sister is addicted to something, you should seek to help. If someone is working an excessive amount of time and neglecting family, then you should come alongside of him to help him. If a man is involved in a relationship that is "shady," then confront him gently. If a sister has missed corporate worship for a month, then she should receive at least a phone call. Be a person who cares for your brothers and sisters, not one who is trying to be everyone's accountability partner. Ultimately, only Jesus can forgive and restore. He puts back together our old broken-down jalopy of a spiritual life. And that is our job, to point others to Jesus. We cannot do this by ignoring sin or remaining silent.

When the woman caught in adultery was brought to Jesus, the people wanted to stone her (John 8:1-11). But Jesus was not interested in destroying this woman; He was interested in restoring her. Be concerned for your broken brother and sister, and like Jesus, lead them to restoration, as they go and sin no more.

The Nature of the Restorer

Paul does not give any "steps for restoration," but he does talk about the *restorer*.

First, the restorer should be spiritual. The idea is that you should not be on a rescue mission if you are not living by the Spirit. Our culture loves to quote Matthew 7:1, "Do not judge, so that you won't be judged," but they are oblivious to Matthew 7:5, "First take the log out of your eye, and then you will see clearly to *take the speck out of your brother's eye*" (emphasis added). Once you take the log out of your eye, then you go take the speck out of your brother's eye. Jesus is not saying to never be concerned for the spiritual welfare of your brother (as the culture often wants to insist). He is urging us to see to our own hearts *first*, and then act. He is ruling out pride. Only the person who humbly repents can go help out those who are struggling. Jesus is opposed to arrogant self-righteousness. He is not opposed to the ministry of restoration performed by a person who is humbly repentant.

Second, the restorer should be gentle. Luther, who is not most remembered for gentleness, once told a pastor charged with setting a lapsed brother back on the right path these words: "Run unto him, and reaching out your hand, raise him up again, comfort him with sweet words, and embrace him with motherly arms" (George, *Galatians*, 412).

Gentleness is a fruit of the Spirit, which implies that such a virtue develops as we abide in Jesus personally. He makes us gentle, like Himself (Matt 11:29).

Third, the restorer should be careful. Paul says, "Watching out for yourselves so you also won't be tempted" (Gal 6:1). Paul told Timothy to "pay close attention to your life and your teaching" (1 Tim 4:16). We must always be aware that we ourselves are not immune to falling. We must *persevere* in guarding our lives.

To what temptation is Paul referring in Galatians 6:1? One of the sins that we must be aware of in the restoration process is spiritual pride. Be careful that you do not exalt yourself over your brother. But Paul seems to be referring to the particular sin itself that has overtaken our brother or sister. Be careful entering a person's world, trying to rescue them. I heard about a guy that went to talk to his friends about their wild drinking parties on the weekends. He had good intentions. He wanted to tell them they do not need alcohol and popular music to escape their problems, but instead they need Jesus. However, he ended up getting drunk himself. Be careful that you do not step in the trap.

So if a person is in sin, restore him or her. Now Paul does not speak to people who are receiving restoration. But just know that sometimes they may not want you to minister to them. Why? Many think that they are independent. But if one is a Christian, he or she is not independent. We are *inter*dependent. We are a body. The whole body of Christ is affected by one another's sin. Your sin always affects others. If you are the one who is being led astray into destructive sin, receive help. It is not only for your good, but for the good of the whole church.

Humble Burden Bearing
GALATIANS 6:2-5

Those who are living in sin need our help (v. 1), and those who are burdened need our help (v. 2). If a Christian brother or sister is weighed down by some burden, then we have a responsibility: do something quickly. Paul writes,

> *Carry one another's burdens; in this way you will fulfill the law of Christ. For if anyone considers himself to be something when he is nothing, he deceives himself. But each person should examine his own work, and then he will have a reason for boasting in himself alone,*

and not in respect to someone else. For each person will have to carry his own load. (Gal 6:2-5)

Do not let your brother get crushed. Be alert and quick to act to ease his or her burden. This is a totally selfless act. That is why we need the Holy Spirit's fruit-bearing work. In our flesh, we are concerned with our burdens. But the Spirit produces love, and that involves caring about our burdened brother or sister.

Perhaps you are wondering, *What should I do with my life?* Here is a daily mission: Be alert to the burdens of others and devote yourself to making them lighter. In addition to the need for the Spirit's work in our lives, what do we need to know in order to do this? Consider six observations on this burden-bearing ministry.

Burdens Are a Reality in a Fallen World (6:2a)

Paul assumes that the Galatians will have burdens. They are unavoidable. They may come in the form of mental illness, physical illness, financial crisis, demonic oppression, addiction, or family crises. But one thing is for sure: no one will escape feeling the weight of such problems. Jesus said, "You will have suffering in this world" (John 16:33).

We Are Not Self-Sufficient (6:2a)

Paul not only assumes that we will have burdens, but that we cannot carry all of our own burdens. Certainly, we must always first cast our burdens on the Lord knowing that He will sustain us (Ps 55:22). And yes, Jesus bore our ultimate burden when He died in our place. But we are also instructed to share our trials and struggles with other believers. Sometimes the answer to our Psalm 55 prayers is found in the help of other believers.

Even the best servants of God need help. Moses was not totally self-sufficient. On one occasion he said, "I can't carry all these people by myself. They are too much for me" (Num 11:14). Jethro told Moses, "What you're doing is not good. . . . [T]he task is too heavy for you. You can't do it alone" (Exod 18:17-18). In 2 Corinthians Paul said that he was weary and afflicted, but the Lord used Titus to help him. He says,

In fact, when we came into Macedonia, we had no rest. Instead, we were troubled in every way: conflicts on the outside, fears inside. But

God, who comforts the humble, comforted us by the arrival of Titus.
(2 Cor 7:5-6)

Even Paul needed support. We all need a Titus at times, and sometimes we need to be the Titus in our brother's or sister's life.

Burden Bearing Is a Command to All Believers (6:2a)

The ministry of burden bearing is not just a suggestion, and it is not reserved for pastors. To be an obedient Christian, operating under the control of the Spirit, we must help others carry their heavy burden. That is what it means to love. That's what it means to be the church.

Burden Bearing Is How We Fulfill the Law of Christ (6:2b)

Stott says, "The 'law of Christ' is to love one another as He loves us; that was the new commandment which he gave" (*Message of Galatians*, 158). Jesus said, "I give you a new command: Love one another. Just as I have loved you, you must also love one another" (John 13:34; cf. 15:12). Stott adds, "It is very impressive that to 'love our neighbor,' 'to bear one another's burdens,' and 'fulfill the law' are three equivalent expressions" (ibid.). We should not be crushed by this command, but should delight in it and realize that we have power to fulfill it through the Spirit's ministry in our lives.

Pride Hinders Burden Bearing (6:3-4)

Paul adds an interesting few sentences saying, "For if anyone considers himself to be something when he is nothing, he deceives himself." What a verse! Some people think they are something. If you think you are above stooping to help your brother, you are deceived. But pride often hinders brotherly love.

This verse reminds me of a story about Muhammad Ali. Allegedly, he was on board a plane and the flight attendant told him to prepare for takeoff by buckling his seatbelt. He shot back, "Superman don't need no seat-belt!" To which she responded, "Superman don't need no airplane! Buckle up!" Do not think of yourself as a spiritual superman. Humble yourself, and serve God's people.

A biblical example of this tendency to elevate self appears in Nehemiah. As the people were working on various parts of the wall, some declined to get involved. The writer says, "their nobles did not lift a finger to help their supervisors" (Neh 3:5). Pride will create a heart that resists humble service to the church family.

Is verse 4 a contradiction of verse 3? Paul says, "But each person should examine his own work, and then he will have a reason for boasting in himself alone, and not in respect to someone else." Is this verse promoting pride? No, it is not. It is not a contradiction of verse 3. Paul basically says not to compare yourself to your neighbor. Instead, examine your own life in view of God's evaluation, and when you do, you will not be so prideful. Do not get puffed up because one is lower than you, either by way of sin, or by way of burden. Paul says to stop feeding your pride by comparing yourself to others. Measure your life by the laws of Christ, and then you will cultivate a humble attitude (cf. 2 Cor 10:12,18).

Paul Distinguishes between Heavy Burdens and Light Loads (6:5)

I could see how someone would think that this verse contradicts verse 2. After Paul says, "Carry one another's burdens" (v. 2), he now says, "For each person will have to carry his own load." So which is it?

The Greek text helps here. Two different words for "burden" are used in these two verses. Paul uses the term *baros* in verse 2, meaning a "weight or heavy load" (Stott, *Message of Galatians*, 159). But he uses the term *phortion* in verse 5, referring to a "man's pack" (ibid.). The latter is translated "load" in HCSB and ESV. The meaning is clear. Some things in life are so heavy we cannot bear them alone. We need help. Other matters in life are the equivalent of what you might carry in a backpack.

Everything in your life is not a crisis. You do not have to call 911 or the National Guard; you do not have to convene a meeting. You need to carry your own backpack. But some things in life are too heavy for you not to ask for help. Do not treat loads as burdens, or burdens as loads.

Consider the following situations and decide which people have "burdens" and which ones have "loads":

A. A young guy, who constantly gets up late for work or school because he stays up playing video games all night, asks you to wake him up every morning so he does not lose his job or flunk out of school.

B. A guy who spends all his money on beer, cigarettes, and lottery tickets refuses to look for a job and asks you for money.

C. A businessman works twelve-hour days, including Saturdays, and asks you to take his son to all of his baseball practices and games.
D. A married couple has three children, and one day there is an accident. One of the parents dies in a car wreck. The remaining parent and the kids have needs.
E. A husband abandons his wife for another woman, leaving her with four kids. She needs help meeting daily responsibilities.
F. An older, faithful church member gets sick and is having a hard time. She needs help with meals, transportation, and occasional living expenses.

(Driscoll, "Open Bibles, Open Lives")

I would argue that situations A-C are in the "loads" category and situations D-F are in the "burdens" category. You need to carry your own load when it comes to responsibilities like going to bed and waking up, working a job and spending money wisely, and raising your kids. But you need help bearing the burden of grief, abandonment, single parenting, and aging.

There are legitimate and illegitimate needs. We must carry our own load, but we must help with burdens. Some treat everything like a load. They refuse to tell anyone or ask for help. That is not healthy. Some treat everything like a burden, occupying hours of people's time with things they should take care of themselves.

I love the scene at the end of the film version of Tolkien's book, *Return of the King*. Frodo is close to completing his task of dropping the evil ring in the fire. But he is too weary and worn to make it up the mountain. Then, his loyal friend Sam says with tears and passion, "Come, Mr. Frodo! I can't carry it for you, but I can carry you." He proceeds to help him up the mountain so Frodo can end the drama once and for all. Spirit-filled believers help their brothers and sisters carry the burdens that crush them.

Generous Sharing
GALATIANS 6:6

In verse 6 Paul shifts gears a bit, saying, "The one who is taught the message must share all his good things with the teacher." Paul speaks to the responsibilities of both the teachers and the receivers within the household of God.

Responsibilities of the Teacher

The teacher must expound the Word of God. The word "taught" and "teacher" both come from the same word, *katecheo*, which is where we get catechism (Stott, *Message of Galatians*, 167). It refers to the fundamentals of the faith. The false teachers deviated from the fundamentals of the faith. They departed from the apostles' teaching, from the word of God.

The role of the pastor-teacher is not to entertain or to use gimmicks to attract people to watch the performance. He is called to teach the truths of Scripture. Why? As a pastor, I am commanded to do so (2 Tim 4:2). But it is also because the Bible is what people need to hear.

Do you belong to a Bible-saturated church? To be sure, teaching is not the only thing the church does. Paul has already mentioned caring for the poor in verse 2:10, and he mentions mercy ministry in 6:10 also. But do not pit these two ministries against each other. We need faithful and effective Bible teachers, and we need people to care for those in need.

Notice also that it is in the context of talking about the Spirit's work that Paul drops this line about teaching. Being a Spirit-led church does not mean avoiding teaching substantively. In the book of Acts, the Spirit was performing amazing wonders, yet the church did not say, "Oh, who needs the Bible?" Instead, we find "they devoted themselves to the apostles' teaching" (Acts 2:42). A Spirit-led church is a teaching church.

Responsibilities of the Receiver

What about the receivers? Obviously, they should learn from their teachers, even re-teaching what they learn, but here Paul focuses on the responsibility to "share all [their] good things" with the one who teaches. Paul urges the believers to support teachers materially. This would include food, money, and whatever good things are appropriate for the teacher's welfare. Paul provided for himself sometimes to keep from burdening the church, but sometimes he did take support, as we see in Philippians and 2 Corinthians 11:8. He thought it was good for the church to support ministers (cf. 1 Cor 9:11-14; 1 Tim 5:17-18).

If Galatians is the earliest epistle, then this is the earliest reference to providing for the minister (George, *Galatians*, 420). While the times have changed, the potential for abuse in this area has not changed. Ministers must avoid *laziness*. Since ministers are often unsupervised most of the day, the temptation is to not work very hard. It is easy to receive a salary and enjoy the security while sowing and sweating very little. That is not living "above reproach" (1 Tim 3:2). Further, ministers must avoid *greed*. When you enter ministry you understand that you will never be wealthy. But once you begin, it is easy to "fall into temptation, a trap, and many foolish and harmful desires" (1 Tim 6:9). Why is it that you rarely hear of pastors feeling called to lower-paying positions in the next phase of their ministries? Resist the love of money. Ministers must also never fall prey to ministerial *professionalism*. Not to be confused with excellence, this temptation is to treat your vocation like any other career. Clock in, clock out. No passion, no desperate prayer, no deep love for people, but all the while serving with a pasted smile and pious words. That is ministerial professionalism, and ministers must avoid it.

Why did Paul include this instruction here? Probably because the teachers in Galatia were in need. Otherwise, I doubt Paul would have mentioned it. Think about it: Paul and Barnabas appointed elders in every church that they planted (Acts 14:23). Maybe the people stopped supporting the ministers that Paul left in Galatia. Maybe they became infatuated with the new theology of the false teachers and stopped supporting those who were accurately catechizing.

Do not miss Paul's ultimate concern; it is not money. Paul's burden was for the furtherance of the gospel, and he knew that the God-ordained means for accomplishing this was the steady proclamation of the Word of God by faithful teachers. But these teachers would be limited if they could not take care of their daily necessities. By caring for the needs of the teacher, the church says, "We want the Word of God taught faithfully and effectively, so we will help support you." Care for those who teach, not out of obligation or tradition, but because you love the Word of God and want to see it spread to the ends of the earth.

Personal Holiness
GALATIANS 6:7-8

Paul has a different emphasis in these verses. He talks about sowing and reaping, but not in relationship to money. It has more to do with personal holiness.

John MacArthur says, "The Christian has only two fields in which he can sow, that of his own flesh and that of the Spirit" (*Galatians*, 188).

This is a divine law: you reap what you sow. If you sow in the Spirit, you will reap the Spirit. If you sow in the flesh, you reap the flesh (5:16-25). To sow to one's flesh is to pander to it, give in to it, and coddle it—instead of crucifying it! The old adage is true: "Sow a thought, reap an act; sow an act, reap a habit; sow a habit, reap a character; sow a character, reap a destiny" (Stott, *Message of Galatians*, 170).

Holiness is a harvest. The seeds are mainly thoughts and deeds. Stott summarizes it powerfully:

> Every time we allow our mind to harbor a grudge, nurse a grievance, entertain an impure fantasy, wallow in self-pity, we are sowing to the flesh. Every time we linger in bad company whose insidious influence we know we cannot resist, every time we lie in bed when we ought to be up and praying, every time we read pornographic literature, every time we take a risk that strains our self-control we are sowing, sowing, sowing, to the flesh. (Ibid.)

Some Christians sow to the flesh every day and wonder why they do not reap holiness and victory and blessing. Let me provide some examples. When a dating couple gets caught up in the sensuality of the moment and engages in sexual activity outside of marriage, then they are sowing to the flesh. When a man fantasizes about taking control of an organization and decides to scheme and cheat to get to the top, then he is sowing seeds of destruction, not only for others, but for his own soul. When a woman secretly despises another woman in the church, without ever seeking reconciliation, she is sowing to the flesh, hurting her own soul and the fellowship of the church. When a husband and wife allow bitterness and resentment to build in marriage without ever trying to resolve their differences and forgive one another, then they are sowing seeds of the flesh, hurting themselves and the whole family. Remember, says Stott, "*Holiness is a harvest*; whether we reap it or not depends almost entirely on what we sow" (ibid., emphasis added).

Paul adds a warning: "God is not mocked." Regardless of who you are, you reap what you sow. Your sin will find you out. Paul says elsewhere, "Their destiny will be according to their works" (2 Cor 11:15). In contrast, those who have been born of the Spirit sow in the Spirit, and they will reap "eternal life" (Gal 6:8).

Choose your field wisely. Sow thoughts and deeds in the Spirit. The books you read, the people you are with, the things you do for entertainment, and the thoughts you possess are acts of sowing. Are they of the flesh or Spirit? When you are sowing in the Spirit, you will reap the reward of the Spirit-controlled life.

How does this relate to biblical community? Simple. What keeps us from restoring our broken brother gently (6:1)? Our failure to sow in the Spirit. Lack of holiness hinders real community. It is the one who is "spiritual" that does the restoring. What keeps us from bearing one another's burdens? It is pride. Where does that come from? It comes from sowing to the flesh. What keeps us from being generous? It is greed. Again, it is a sowing to the flesh. Why will we not "work for the good of . . . the household of faith" (v. 10)? It is because we are too occupied with ourselves. Lack of personal holiness does damage to the family of faith.

Practical Goodness
GALATIANS 6:9-10

Paul concludes the section by offering some encouragement in verse 9 and an instruction on biblical community in verse 10. His **encouragement** is this: "So we must not get tired of doing good, for we will reap at the proper time if we don't give up." Compassionate ministry can make you weary. Contending for the gospel can make you exhausted. Every Christian can become discouraged in doing good deeds. So Paul says, Keep sowing. Continue loving one another. Keep resisting bickering with others. Keep rejecting false teachers. Keep bearing one another's burdens. Keep preaching the gospel. Keep doing good, and watch God work. There is a harvest out there! We reap what we sow, even though it may take years before you see fruit (as in the case with William Carey!), but it is worth it.

Remember also that even though the phrase "at the proper time" may be appropriately applied to this life, we should also note the future time. The larger application is that we will reap reward for faithfulness to God in the eschatological future (George, *Galatians*, 426). No deed is small in this life. Keep serving faithfully.

Finally, consider Paul's specific instruction, "Therefore, as we have opportunity, we must *work for the good* of all, especially for those who belong to the household of faith" (v. 10, emphasis added). Believers should be marked by practical goodness.

Notice the universal and particular challenge. *Universally,* we must love our neighbor as ourselves. We should be sensitive to the poor in our community. We look for ways to show mercy to "all," to those around the world who have urgent physical needs.

Particularly, Paul says that we pay careful attention to those in "the household of faith." Look for opportunities to "work for the good" everywhere among the fellowship. Love your neighbor sensitively. But pay special attention to ways you can do good to those within the church. That may mean restoring a broken brother, bearing burdens, supporting your teacher, helping with transportation, paying a bill for someone who lost his or her job, tutoring that struggling kid, or baby-sitting for parents so they can have a date night. Look for ways to bless those in the household of faith.

Put the whole section together now. Let us be a Spirit-led people marked by gentle restoration, humble burden bearing, generous sharing, personal holiness, and practical goodness.

This is life in the Spirit. Were these qualities not embodied in Jesus? Yes, perfectly. Jesus restored us from our broken relationship with God. He continues to restore our souls. He carried our greatest burden, the crushing weight of sin. He kept God's law in our place, and then died in our place, removing the penalty of sin that was upon us, so that there is now no condemnation for those who are in Christ Jesus. Jesus is the ultimate generous giver, who made us rich through His poverty (2 Cor 8:9). Jesus constantly sowed in the Spirit, lived a life of perfect righteousness, and reaped eternal glory. Jesus was a prophet mighty in word and deed, who "went about doing good" (Acts 10:38). Jesus gives us the example, and He gives us the Spirit to live out these responsibilities.

Reflect and Discuss

1. What sets the church apart from other, charitable organizations and clubs, even religious ones?
2. How does the discussion about the "fruit of the Spirit" (5:16-26) relate to this passage (6:1-10)?
3. Have you ever needed to restore a brother gently? If so, what was that like? Do you need to do so now? How should you go about it?
4. How is confronting the sin of other believers different from Jesus' command, "Do not judge" (Matt 7:1)?
5. What are some examples of how one might "carry one another's burdens"? What might hinder this from happening?

6. What is the difference between "burdens" and "loads" (6:2,5)?
7. How is holiness a harvest?
8. Are you getting tired of doing good (6:9)? If so, how might you find fresh strength?
9. Are you looking for an "opportunity" to bless others? In what ways might you do that today?
10. Based on the truths in this text, how would you answer the following question: "If I study Scripture, pray, and listen to sermons throughout the week, why do I need the church?"

Boasting in the Cross

GALATIANS 6:11-18

Main Idea: Paul summarizes some of the major themes of the letter as he contrasts his cross-centered ministry with the self-exalting ministry of the false teachers.

I. **A Cross-Centered Conclusion (6:11)**
II. **Cross-Centered Contrasts (6:12-18)**
   A. A cross-centered life is humble not prideful (6:12-13).
   B. A cross-centered life boasts in the cross not self (6:14a).
   C. A cross-centered life treasures Christ not the world (6:14b).
   D. A cross-centered life values spiritual transformation not external ritual (6:15-16).
   E. A cross-centered life walks in truth not error (6:16).
   F. A cross-centered life seeks to please Christ not man (6:17-18).

Fashion trends fascinate me. Have you been intrigued by a few clothing items recently? As bizarre as some things are today, my generation has also worn some crazy things. Remember the '80s? Some of you are trying to put that out of your mind. The music, the jams with matching tank tops, British Knights sneakers, spandex shorts, hammer pants, Raiders football gear, tight rolled pants, overalls with one flap down. And what about those hairstyles? Guys wore mullets, and ladies were walking fire hazards with all that hairspray on those bangs!

My parents' days were not much better. My photo album contains pictures of leisure suits, waterfall haircuts, and later, very short coach's shorts. All of this is proof that we live in a fallen world!

Of all the strange things that people wear, what do you think the disciples would have considered the strangest? It would not be any of these items. It would have to be *a cross*. While a cross is a symbol of our faith, in the first century it was an instrument of death. Crucifixion was the most cruel and agonizing means of execution ever devised. It was designed and then refined by the Romans not just to kill, but also to degrade and humiliate. Imagine hanging whipped and naked on a cross with spikes in your arms and legs while everyone walked by and spat on you and cursed you. We don't have anything like this today, so we can't understand the horror and shock that wearing an accessory like a cross necklace would bring. In fact, crucifixion was so bad that the Romans would not execute any Roman citizen in this manner. So when it comes down to it, wearing a cross is like wearing a gold chain with a charm representing an electric chair, a gas chamber, or a lynch mob.

The Jews had despised the cross for centuries: "Everyone who is hung on a tree is cursed" (Gal 3:13; cf. Deut 21:23). Consider then the strangeness of,

> But as for me, I will never boast about anything except the cross of
> our Lord Jesus Christ. The world has been crucified to me through the
> cross, and I to the world. (6:14)

Paul says that we should not boast in anything except this instrument of torture. Or to say it positively, we should only boast in the cross. But it is not strange when you consider one particular crucified man who died on a cross. When you know the significance of Jesus' death, then you can agree with Paul's desire. Apart from the cross, we have none of the benefits of salvation.

This may be my favorite verse in the New Testament. Spurgeon said Galatians 6:14 "was the theme of [Paul's] ministry" ("Three Crosses"). Paul was radically cross-centered. He stands in contrast to the false teachers of Galatia, who were self-centered. Paul preached a Christ-given righteousness, accomplished through His finished work. The false teachers preached a works-based righteousness, accomplished through human performance. Paul is a "Christ-exalter," and the false teachers are "self-exalters." Let us consider how we too might live a Christ-exalting, cross-centered life.

A Cross-Centered Conclusion
GALATIANS 6:11

In these final verses, Paul touches on some of the major themes of the letter, and they center on this one big theme: the cross. Here, "the Galatians are reminded as to what is at stake in this controversy" (Schreiner, *Galatians*, 373). Indeed, Galatians is about a controversy. (Interestingly, virtually every letter in the NT is written because of a controversy!) The controversy in Galatians is about the nature of salvation. Paul is making one final plea that "Jesus paid it all." The false teachers thought that what Jesus did was not enough. So Paul pleads one more time with emotion, like a lawyer making his final appeal to a judge and jury, that they would realize that Christ's work is enough.

Before we go through these applications note verse 11. "Look at what large letters I use as I write to you in my own handwriting." I do not think that "large letters" refers to Paul having poor eyesight or means that his hands are deformed. Rather, the large letters signify the importance of what is described. Paul takes the reed pen from his scribe and writes the conclusion in bold script.

Elsewhere, Paul ends with his signature (1 Cor 16:21; Col 4:18; 2 Thess 3:17), but here he adds *more* than his signature. The closing comments are much longer than in his other letters (6:12-15). The benediction is different also; it is conditional (v. 16). The tone of verse 17 is different; it is sharp. Even though Paul gives a prayer wish, there are no personal greetings from others and no expression of praise or thanksgiving in the conclusion.

So the conclusion is very important. He writes passionately with big letters about what was big to him: the cross. Now let us consider six marks of a cross-centered life (with credit to Danny Akin for the outline).

Cross-Centered Contrasts
GALATIANS 6:12-18

1: A Cross-Centered Life Is Humble Not Prideful (6:12-13)

Look at the false religion promoted by these false teachers. The false teachers were motivated by self-interest and their own agenda. Consider the expressions of pride noted by Paul here. Paul says that they were *manipulators*, who "compel." They were *compromisers*, who wanted to "avoid being persecuted." They were *hypocrites*, who "don't keep the law themselves." They were *braggers*, who loved to "boast."

The false teachers wanted to avoid persecution from Jewish opponents. These opponents apparently would not persecute them as long as they followed the law. In addition, they wanted the adulation of others. Paul's words remind us of Jesus' words to the Pharisees. He criticized them for not keeping the law themselves, for their self-centered motives, and for desiring the praise of others (Matt 23). So, here again is the question in the letter: Is true faith, true religion, about divine accomplishment or human achievement? If it is about human achievement, then praise the person; if it is about divine accomplishment, then praise Jesus.

For us, the application is clear. Either you glory in the flesh or you glory in the Christ. Pick one. Our culture is wrapped up with boasting. We exalt popularity, intellect, appearance, income, or job performance, just to name a few. Paul, however, says there is only one acceptable form of boast, only in "the cross." As he wrote to the Corinthians, "The one who boasts must boast in the Lord" (1 Cor 1:31).

The circumcision party is wrapped up in religious boasting. They were religious show-offs. This word "good impression" *(euprosopein)* is found nowhere else in the New Testament. Cole writes, "Paul's point was that the Jews wanted ecclesiastical statistics; so many circumcisions in a given year was certainly something to boast about" (in George, *Galatians,* 433). Sounds like the religious bragging at pastors' conferences! A cross-centered life is one that rejects the model of these false teachers.

Are you cultivating humility in your life and trying to crucify human pride? How can you do this? You must go to the cross. At the cross, our pride bubble gets popped. There is no room for boasting at Golgotha. We must crucify the flesh and walk by the Spirit to cultivate humility and avoid the false teacher's pattern.

Edmund Clowney provides an excellent illustration of ministerial humility:

> On one occasion I had tea with Martyn Lloyd-Jones in London, and decided to ask him a question that concerned me. "Dr. Lloyd-Jones," I said, "How can I tell whether I am preaching in the energy of the flesh or in the power of the Spirit?"
> "That is very easy," Lloyd-Jones replied, as I shriveled. "If you are preaching in the energy of the flesh, you will feel exalted and lifted up. If you are preaching in the power of the Spirit, you will feel awe and humility." (*Preaching Christ in All of Scripture,* 55)

Do you feel exalted and lifted up or in awe and humility before Christ? How we must learn to rely on the Spirit in life and in ministry!

2: A Cross-Centered Life Boasts in the Cross Not Self (6:14a)

Paul says, I will not boast in myself; I will boast in someone and something else. He says, "But as for me, I will never boast about anything except the cross of our Lord Jesus Christ." When Paul says, "I will never," he uses that Greek expression *me genoito*, the strongest Greek negative he could use (cf. Rom 6:1-2). He is trying to find absolute language to emphasize this point: Do not ever boast in anything except the cross. To put it positively, only boast in the cross. *Boast* means to "glory in," "make much of," "be consumed with," or "be mastered by" something. It is deep. It comes from your center, from your soul. The psalmist says, "We boast in God all day long; we will praise Your name forever" (Ps 44:8). May it never be that we would ever make much of anything, or ever glory in anything, or be mastered by anything, except the cross!

Boasting in the cross implies that you place your confidence in Christ and His work for your salvation. You are not trusting in your religious acts. Cross-exalters rest everything in what Christ has done. Cross-exalters believe that Jesus lived the life we could not live and died the death we should have died. Those who boast in the cross simply say, "This is for my peace: Jesus died in my place." Boasting in the cross implies that God accepts you because of the work of Christ. You can say, "Because of the cross, the wrath of God will not be poured out on me. Because of the cross, I am united to Christ. Because of the cross, I am dead to this world and all its claims on my life. Because of the cross, I have become a new creation." So boast in the cross. Revel in it. Rejoice in it.

Boast only in the cross because every spiritual blessing you enjoy or will enjoy is due to the cross. Everything we enjoy as new creations is owing to the cross. Do you enjoy justification? Boast in the cross. Do you enjoy redemption? Boast in the cross. Do you enjoy adoption? Boast in the cross. Do you enjoy the Spirit? Boast in the cross.

3: A Cross-Centered Life Treasures Christ Not the World (6:14b)

The cross has a present power in our lives. The cross has the power to free us from the world's bondage. "The world" speaks of the system and nature of this age. Corruption, meaninglessness, hopelessness, futility, warped values, and despair are all aspects of this world. Paul says the believer and the world are dead to each other! The two have parted ways.

Our position in one sense, objectively, forensically, is this: we have been crucified already with Jesus. We belong to Him (5:24). The best way to understand this phrase in 14b is, "I have been crucified with Christ" (2:19). So we died. But we live. There is a new "I." The old self has died—the rebellious, enslaved, unbelieving self died. Now there is a new "I," a new creation.

Paul wants us to know that when Christ died, we died to the world, and now we live a new life in Him. It does not mean that the world does not affect us. The deathblow has been dealt at the cross, but the world still has a lingering influence. One day, though, when Christ returns, there will be no more corruption. Now the Christian life is about becoming what we are! We are dead to this world and alive to Christ. The world is not the believer's treasure, Christ is.

On account of the cross, the cares of this world do not have to crush us because we have a different perspective than the world. You know that if God will give you Christ, He will give all you need ultimately. The enticements of the world do not have to persuade us like they do the rest of society because we have new affections. Greed can be replaced by generosity; lust with purity; anxiety with truth; envy with love.

Paul says, "Live this out! Live as though this world has nothing for you and Christ is everything to you! Die to the enticements and cares of this world, and live as though Christ were your ultimate treasure. The motto for the Christian is: the world has nothing for us; Christ is everything to us. This is the daily power of the cross."

Charles Spurgeon, in a sermon called "Grand Glorying," writes these amazing words:

> What means he by this? Why, he means that ever since he fell in love with Jesus Christ, he lost all love for the world! It seemed to him to be a poor, crucified, dying thing, and he turned away from it just as you would from a criminal whom you might see hanging in chains—and would desire to go anywhere rather than see the poor being. So Paul seemed to see the world on gallows—hung up there. "There," he said, "that is what I think of you and all your pomp, and all your power, and all your wealth, and all your fame! You are on the gallows, a malefactor, nailed up, crucified! I would not give a fig for you!" . . . And now observe the other Cross. There is Paul on that. The world thinks as little of Paul as Paul does of the world. The world says, "Oh, the harebrained Paul! He was once sensible, but he has gone mad upon that stubborn notion about the Crucified one! The man is a fool." So the world crucifies him. . . . So is it with the world and the genuine Christian.

Can you look at your idols—money, success, human praise, power, peer approval, wanting attention, ungodly romance—and say, "I would not give a fig for you"? See your idols for what they are: pathetic, crucified, dying things. They are not attractive to the person who sees them for what they are and sees Jesus for all He is.

Can you accept that you will be different from the world if you live out this verse? Others may deem you "crazy" or "foolish." So be it. Treasure Jesus, not the world. The cross gives us the power to do just that.

4: A Cross-Centered Life Values Spiritual Transformation Not External Ritual (6:15-16)

The cross has done for us what the flesh could not do. It has done what law-keeping could not do. Christ has made us new people through His work on the cross. Earlier Paul said that circumcision or uncircumcision does not accomplish anything, only "faith working through love" matters (5:6). In other words, he values internal change not external ritual. Now he says something similar:

> For both circumcision and uncircumcision mean nothing; what matters instead is a new creation. (6:15)

This verse reflects what Paul says in 2 Corinthians 5:14-21, where he ties the cross to the new creation. In that letter he says, "Therefore, if anyone is in Christ, he is a new creation; old things have passed away, and look, new things have come" (2 Cor 5:17).

What does a new creation look like? Look at Galatians 2:19-20. These wonderful verses put boasting in the cross and a new creation together. A person who is united to Jesus Christ, who died on his behalf, is never the same person again! He has become a new creation!

Are you glad this is true? Are you glad that you are a new creation? Christianity is not about being a nice person, trying harder, or just being religious. It is about becoming a new person. And this new life is made possible by the cross.

As new creations in Christ, we are now fit for *a new creation.* The new creation has dawned with the coming of Christ. We live between the times of His comings. We will enjoy the blessing of the new creation because of the cross.

Circumcision or new creation? Paul says only the latter represents biblical Christianity. You may perform all sorts of religious rituals, but none of it matters if you have not become a new creation in Christ. Many people today think that there are only two ways to live. They believe that they can either be religious or irreligious. They think that they have to keep a set of rules, or they can live free of rules, like a hedonist. Most irreligious people think that when you are calling them to Christ, you are calling them to religion. But the gospel is something else. It is a third way. It is not about religious acts. It is not primarily a code of ethics. It is an explosion. It is about being united to Christ, who then works in His followers, empowering them to live differently.

5: A Cross-Centered Life Walks in Truth Not Error (6:16)

Paul says this new gospel community, called the church, walks by a "standard." The word "standard" is *kanon*, which means a measuring rod or carpenter's rule. It is the word we use for "canon of Scripture," the 66 books of the Bible. In this context, the standard is the message of the cross and new creation.

Timothy George summarizes this verse: "[Paul] invokes the peace and mercy of God upon those . . . who remain faithful to the truth of the gospel Paul had originally preached among them" (*Galatians*, 439). Danny Akin says, "Once more this reminds us that theology matters; that theology is important; that good, sound gospel-centered theology is essential to both the health and life of the church. Ultimately this is something for which the whole church is responsible" ("The Cross and Faithful Ministry").

Indeed, Paul is passionate about his people walking in, not just affirming intellectually, the truth of the gospel. This is made evident in Paul's words about Peter "deviating from the truth of the gospel" (2:14).

His blessing of "peace . . . and mercy" is the opposite of the "curse" he desired for those who taught false gospels, as mentioned in the beginning of the letter (1:8-9). We should also note that in the church we find peace when we walk in the gospel, and we can experience mercy and show mercy when we saturate ourselves with the gospel. Gospel-centered people should be a mercy-dispensing, peace-enjoying people. Paul refers to the "Israel of God" as the new community of faith. Peace and mercy may come to Gentile and Jew alike, as they embrace the gospel.

"Follow" is the same word in 5:25. Paul is urging us to keep in step with this teaching. Let me encourage you to walk according to the gospel, to walk according to the Spirit. Keep in step with the gospel, not the world.

6: A Cross-Centered Life Seeks to Please Christ Not Man (6:17-18)

Paul concludes by first saying, "From now on, let no one cause me trouble, because I bear on my body scars for the cause of Jesus." What does he mean by "let no one cause me trouble"? Paul basically means, "I will not allow myself to be troubled, harassed, or bothered by the agendas and rules of people, especially these false teachers." Instead, Paul lives for someone else: Jesus. He can say, "I am scarred by Him." His goal, as mentioned earlier, was to please God, not people (1:10).

The Scars (v. 17). The word for "scars" is *stigmata*—the spots or marks. Paul is referring to the wounds he received from following Jesus. He mentions "far worse beatings" (2 Cor 11:23-25). These scars were the scars of Jesus. The word *stigmata* was used for the branding of slaves; Paul was branded. He was Christ's slave. He was Christ's bondservant. As a Jew, he had the mark that the Judaizers were emphasizing, circumcision, but he says the real mark is suffering for Christ. Others wanted to boast in this ritual of circumcision; Paul could say, "Let me show you a physical mark of devotion: Look at my back!"

Unlike the Judaizers, he had not avoided persecution by preaching a false gospel (5:11). He was a faithful messenger, a scarred messenger.

In Luke the same verb "bear" is used of disciples who must bear their own cross (Luke 14:27). John uses the word for Jesus carrying His cross to His execution (John 19:17). If you are going to follow Jesus, you are going to bear some scars. You will bleed, if not in the body, then in the heart. Paul tells Timothy, "In fact, all those who want to live a godly life in Christ Jesus will be persecuted" (2 Tim 3:12). This does not mean we go looking for trouble; it simply means we should be ready and not surprised if we suffer for Christ's sake. Jesus never promises us that life will be easy and devoid of hardship, but He does promise that He will be with us! And He is worth it!

This passage shows us Paul's great love for the Savior. He not only bore the spiritual marks of a believer, he also bore literal scars for his obedience to Jesus. This verse reflects Christ's call to all of us:

> *Summoning the crowd along with His disciples, He said to them, "If anyone wants to be My follower, he must deny himself, take up his cross, and follow Me. For whoever wants to save his life will lose it, but whoever loses his life because of Me and the gospel will save it. For what does it benefit a man to gain the whole world yet lose his life? What can a man give in exchange for his life? For whoever is ashamed*

of Me and of My words in this adulterous and sinful generation, the Son of Man will also be ashamed of him when He comes in the glory of His Father with the holy angels." (Mark 8:34-38)

Grace Be with You (v. 18). Notice the appropriate ending to this letter: Grace. He began with customary salutation of grace (1:3). He has spoken of being called by grace and the necessity of believing in the gospel of grace. The whole letter is about the grace of Jesus, God's unmerited favor on sinners. Christ dying for us, Christ justifying us, Christ redeeming us, Christ adopting us, the Spirit indwelling us, the church helping us—all of it is grace.

Now he says, "Brothers, the grace of our Lord Jesus Christ be with your spirit. Amen." Here is the sum and substance of a disciple: the marks of Jesus on your body and the grace of Jesus in your spirit.

The term "brothers" shows us how disciples are not alone. The grace of God revealed in the gospel of Jesus has not only changed our relationship with God; it has also changed our relationship with people. God forms a family through the gospel.

Now may grace be multiplied to us as we live cross-centered lives! Such a life is reflected well in this beloved hymn:

> When I survey the wondrous cross
> On which the Prince of glory died,
> My richest gain I count but loss,
> And pour contempt on all my pride.
>
> Forbid it, Lord, that I should boast,
> Save in the death of Christ my God!
> All the vain things that charm me most,
> I sacrifice them to His blood.
>
> See from His head, His hands, His feet,
> Sorrow and love flow mingled down!
> Did e'er such love and sorrow meet,
> Or thorns compose so rich a crown?
>
> His dying crimson, like a robe,
> Spreads o'er His body on the tree;
> Then I am dead to all the globe,
> And all the globe is dead to me.

Were the whole realm of nature mine,
That were a present far too small;
Love so amazing, so divine,
Demands my soul, my life, my all.
(Watts, "When I Survey the Wondrous Cross")

Reflect and Discuss

1. How does Paul speak of the hypocrisy of the false teachers in these verses? How does legalism lead to hypocrisy?
2. In what possessions, gifts, and opportunities are you tempted to boast? How does the message of the cross change your perspective?
3. What does it mean to boast in the cross? How can you boast in the cross practically every day?
4. Why might proclaiming the cross bring persecution?
5. How does Paul say the cross should affect our view of the world?
6. Do you think many people perceive Christianity as "being nice" instead of "becoming a new creation"? How does the latter change everything?
7. What does Paul mean by "follow this standard" (v. 16)? How does this relate to Paul's confrontation of Peter (2:14)?
8. How do "peace" and "mercy" relate to the gospel?
9. How is Christ's death on the cross unique and unrepeatable? How is it a pattern for His followers?
10. What role should the cross play in a gospel presentation? Be specific.

WORKS CITED

Akin, Daniel L. "The Cross and Faithful Ministry." Accessed September 2, 2013. http://www.danielain.com/wp-content/uploads/2010/08/Galatians-6.11-18-The-Cross-And-Faithful-Ministry-As-Seen-In-The-Pastoral-And-Missionary-Ministry-Of-George-Leile-Manuscript-ds1.pdf.

Barrett, C. K. *The First Epistle to the Corinthians.* In Black's New Testament Commentary. Third Printing. Peabody: Hendrickson, 2000.

Burke, Trevor. *Adoption into God's Family.* Downers Grove: InterVarsity, 2006.

Corbett, Steve, and Brian Fikkert. *When Helping Hurts.* Chicago: Moody, 2009.

Clowney, Edmund. *Preaching Christ in All of Scripture.* Wheaton: Crossway, 2003.

Dallimore, Arnold A. *George Whitefield.* Volume 1. Carlisle: Banner of Truth Trust, 1970.

Dever, Mark. "The Church Is the Gospel Made Visible." Accessed September 1, 2013. http://t4g.org/media/2010/06/the-church-is-the-gospel-made-visible-session-i-3.

Driscoll, Mark. "Open Bibles, Open Lives." Accessed March 3, 2012. http://marshill.com/media/galatians/open-bibles-open-lives.

Edwards, Jonathan. "Christian Charity," accessed August 31, 2013. http://www.biblebb.com/files/edwards/charity.htm.

Forde, Gerhard. "The Lutheran View." In *Christian Spirituality.* Edited by Donald Alexander. Downers Grove: InterVarsity Press, 1988.

George, Timothy. *Galatians.* The New American Commentary. Nashville: B&H, 1994.

Gilbert, Greg. *What Is the Gospel?* Wheaton: Crossway, 2010.

Grudem, Wayne. *Systematic Theology.* Grand Rapids: Zondervan, 1994.

Keller, Tim. *Center Church.* Grand Rapids: Zondervan, 2012.

———. *Generous Justice.* New York: Dutton, 2010.

———. "Getting Out." Accessed March 1, 2013. http://thegospelcoalition.org/resources/entry/getting_out,

———. *Prodigal God.* New York: Dutton, 2008.

———. "Rescue," accessed September 10, 2011. http://sermons.redeemer.com/store/index.cfm?fuseaction=product.display&product_ID=18298.

———. "The Centrality of the Gospel." Accessed February 1, 2013. http://sermons.redeemer.com/store/index.cfm?fuseaction=product.display&product_ID=17858&ParentCat=6.

Lewis, C. S. *Four Loves.* In *The Inspirational Writings of C. S. Lewis.* Originally published 1960; reprt., New York: Inspirational Press, 1994.

———. *Mere Christianity.* Originally published 1952; repr., New York: HarperCollins, 2000,

Luther, Martin. *A Commentary on St. Paul's Epistle to the Galatians.* Philadelphia: Smith, English & Co., 1860.

———. *Lectures on Galatians.* Translated and edited by Jaroslav Pelikan. Vols. 26–27 in Luther's Works. St. Louis: Concordia, 1963.

Mahaney, C. J. *Living the Cross Centered Life.* Colorado Springs: Multnomah, 2006.

Moore, Russell. *Adopted for Life.* Wheaton: Crossway, 2009.

Morris, Leon. *Galatians: Paul's Charter of Christian Freedom.* Downers Grove: InterVarsity Press, 1996.

Packer, J. I. *Knowing God.* Downers Grove: InterVarsity, 1973.

Piper, John. "Adoption: The Heart of the Gospel." Accessed October 1, 2010. http://www.desiringgod.org/resource-library/conference-messages/adoption-the-heart-of-the-gospel.

———. "Christ Redeemed Us from the Curse of the Law." Accessed September 27, 2013. http://www.desiringgod.org/resource-library/sermons/christ-redeemed-us-from-the-curse-of-the-law.

———. "Only a New Creation Counts." Accessed August 12, 2013. http://www.desiringgod.org/resource-library/sermons/only-a-new-creation-counts,

Quintilian, Marcus Fabius. *The Institutio oratoria of Quintilian.* Volume 1. Translated by H. E. Butler. London: W. Heinemann, 1920.

Rosner, Brian S. "Known by God." Accessed August 24, 2013. http://www.biblicalstudies.org.uk/pdf/eq/2005-4_343.pdf.

Rutherford, Samuel L. *The Loveliness of Christ.* Accessed September 1, 2013. http://mediadownload.radiantwebtools.com/communitychristianministries/Articles%2Floveliness_2012.pdf.

Schreiner, Tom. *Galatians*. Zondervan Exegetical Commentary on the New Testament. Grand Rapids: Zondervan, 2010.

Sproul, R. C. *Essential Truths of the Christian Faith*. Carol Stream: Tyndale, 1992.

Spurgeon, Charles. "All of Grace." Accessed September 6, 2013. http://www.spurgeon.org/sermons/3479.htm.

———. "A Sermon and a Reminiscence." Accessed Sept 1, 2012. http://www.spurgeon.org/s_and_t/srmn1873.htm.

———. "Non Nobis, Domine." Accessed August 20, 2013. http://www.spurgeongems.org/vols46-48/chs2784.pdf.

———. "Three Crosses." Accessed September 4, 2013. http://www.spurgeongems.org/vols22-24/chs1447.pdf.

Stott, John R. W. *The Message of Galatians*. The Bible Speaks Today. Downers Grove: InterVarsity, 1986.

Tchividjian, Tullian. *Jesus + Nothing = Everything*. Wheaton: Crossway, 2011.

———. "Then I Will Go with You." Accessed March 3, 2013. http://thegospelcoalition.org/blogs/tullian/2011/01/22/then-i-will-go-with-you.

Watson, Thomas. *The Doctrine of Repentance*. Originally published in 1660. Reprinted Carlisle: Banner of Truth, 1987.

Westminster Shorter Catechism, available online at http://www.reformed.org/documents/index.html?mainframe=http://www.reformed.org/documents/WSC_frames.html.

Whitecross, John. "The Shorter Catechism Illustrated." Accessed September 6, 2013. http://www.shortercatechism.com/resources/whitecross/wsc_wh_035.html.

SCRIPTURE INDEX